New Beginnings

THE HOWARD AND BUZZIE STORY

SHARON HOLETON LARSEN

authorHOUSE®

AuthorHouse™
1663 Liberty Drive
Bloomington, IN 47403
www.authorhouse.com
Phone: 1 (800) 839-8640

Published by AuthorHouse 09/03/2019

ISBN: 978-1-7283-2588-0 (sc)
ISBN: 978-1-7283-2587-3 (e)

Print information available on the last page.

This book is printed on acid-free paper.

Part One

The little tar paper house sat on the northeast corner of Bear Lake Road where it intersected with old 26 Road. If you walked far enough north past the little tar paper house on old 26 you would get to Howard and Buzzies place, the one they called the farm. Two elderly people lived in the black tar paper house all the time and sometimes they had lots of other people living with them, mostly children. The little woman had long white hair that she wound up in a bun each day, until her daughters decided to modernize her and started giving her permanents in her later years. She was short and barrel shaped and had the darkest eyes, cow eyes people would say. It was told to me that she was half French and half Spanish, as if that were to explain her looks. She had a very rough life according to the story. She gave birth to eleven children and raised nine of them to adulthood, but in actuality she raised many more. Half of her grandchildren lived with her, some of them for many years. She never seemed sad to me, always a ready smile and a big hug for everyone. This little old lady named Ida.

The old man from the tar paper house was really tall. He had white hair on his head and his chin and I never saw him without a pipe in his mouth. He talked real tough and mean, most of the time and people said that's how he was. In fact some would say he was the meanest man who had ever lived. They said he beat his boys constantly while they were growing up. He made them all quit school in the fifth or sixth grade and go to work in the lumber camps with him. That was the way he made a living and pressured his three sons to do the same. It was the only way he knew!

His daughters all ran away at fourteen or fifteen and married just to escape his beatings. Most of those marriages lasted all their lives. The story was, one day he quit beating them because he hurt Ida real bad when she got between him, his belt and whatever child he was beating. He never picked up his belt again.

Whatever stories I heard about his meanness didn't apply to me because I loved him, this loud talking, white haired Grandpa TJ. In fact Ida and TJ were my favorite people in the whole world. My first memories of them start at three or four years old and run on for a lot of years. They always called me the runt of the litter and to me it sounded special.

Behind Ida and T.J.'s house the land seemed to go straight uphill. You had to walk up several wooden steps to get to the outhouse or garden and go up to that garden, is what I loved to do. How many hundreds of times I must have climbed up those wooden steps to find T.J. in his garden. People used to say no one was allowed in his garden but for some reason, unknown to me, I was.

I would follow him around asking all sorts of puzzling questions, like "Why do you live out here in your garden?" I had no doubt heard the grownups say that about him. Someone was always saying ole T. J. just lives in the garden. He had his reasons, TJ would say, for one, he hated weeds and would spend hours pulling them. For another, the soil had to be just right around his plants, if it was too tightly packed the plants couldn't grow up strong and healthy and if the soil was too loose, the plants went wild and spread out too much. Sometimes TJ would answer me by saying he wanted to get closer to God. He would say that man is closer to God in his garden than anywhere else on earth. In my little pea brain I figured that just climbing those stairs up to the garden brought us closer to God.

Ida and TJ were very poor and had to count on their children to help them out. Eventually their children did help them, with the house at least. The tarpaper got covered with some brown stuff that almost looked like brick. A wire got strung from the road and gave them electricity instead of the oil burning lamps. Years later they even had a telephone installed. They never replaced the out house though and for all her days Ida cooked on the big wood burning stove in the main part of their house. Oh, how she cooked, and baked. That house always smelled like fresh bread and coffee.

I wonder if anyone ever entered Ida and TJ's house without having coffee. People would pour out their troubles to Ida and she would pour out the coffee and listen to them. TJ would just grumble and go off by himself. He spent a lot of time sitting in the living room reading his bible and smoking his pipe, or out in his garden.

A lot of grandchildren's lives took direction in that little three room shack with its unheated attic. Mine was no exception. I will never forget the day a cookie was missing from Ida's pantry. When I confessed that I had taken it, I thought Ida was going to cry. She made me feel so ashamed, for she said to take without asking was stealing, and did I want to be a thief? Oh no, I didn't want to be a thief. TJ said, at least I wasn't a liar. I promised them, I promised myself and I promised God I would never take anything ever again without asking.

Ida and TJ had seven daughters and four sons. Howard was their third son, born somewhere in the middle of their eleven children. He was tall like his father and tough sounding like him too. Still he had some of Grandma Ida's ways in him, like her dark, dark eyes and her soft heart.

Howard would give you anything he had if he felt you needed it, and he would go without eating himself if it looked like there wasn't enough food to go around. The worst thing about Howard, from my point of view, was his filthy mouth. He never even said a simple statement like, its a nice day outside without injecting swear words into it. Perhaps those stories about having to quit school so young or living with tough lumberjacks at such an early age---I don't know! I just know it hurt me bad, it hurt my heart, to hear him swear. I felt like every one would know he was unschooled since instead of using the right words, he used cuss words in all his conversations.

It hurt me doubly bad when he used my Gods name in his swearing. Yes, some how it was my God, how the Lord got to be my God is unknown to me. Was is from TJ reading his bible and talking about it or was it instilled in me at the tender age of two or three when I had lived with Buzzie's parents. They were real God fearing people and took me to church always and read the bible every night. I don't know! I just know it was my God, and to hear that gentle giant of a man use

Buzzie

Ida & TJ

Punky & Sharie

All at Ida & TJ's House about 1941

SPECIAL   get-togethers

Howard with his 2 brothers

7

my Gods name in cursing hurt my heart. Howards swearing would bother me every time he talked and yet.....I don't remember ever telling him so.

In May, in his twenty-first year on this earth, Howard married Buzzie. She was seventeen and pregnant at the time. There are so many stories planted in my brain about those early years that I have no knowledge of what really happen. No way of knowing if any, or what part of any of them are true so to repeat them would serve no purpose. The facts were only known to Howard and Buzzie.

The way Buzzie told the story to me was, it was love at first sight. She was a friend of one of Howard's sisters and was with the sister this particular day. Buzzie and her friend were watching some guys play baseball. When Buzzie accidently dropped something over the fence, this tall, good looking guy came and picked it up for her. She was smitten right then and asked her friend all about her brother, the handsome Howard. Can you believe she dropped an object again just to see if he would repeat his gallant pick up and delivery, (sounds like the old handkerchief trick). Buzzie decided then and there, that was the man she would marry.

The details of their courtship are not known by me, I only know they married in May of 1936 and had a son, Punky, the day after Christmas. On Halloween night two years later I was born. Most everyone who ever met Howard and Buzzie said they should never have had children. They were vagabonds and would move on a whim. Sometimes with us kids, more often without us. They were always making a new start, a new beginning, mostly because they wanted to escape a love affair one of them had just ended.

Yes, they changed partners almost as often as they changed houses. The children were left by Grandparents, friends, Aunts or Uncles or when they were big enough to go to school they would be left alone. Howard and Buzzie would promise to send for or come and get the children as soon as they could find a new house or new jobs. It always took so much longer than they planned and us kids would wait and wonder if they would ever come back. When they would come back it was wonderful. I loved them so much! There was always this renewed hope of a normal life. I savor the good times. We all laughed and cried, and we sang. Was anyone ever so happy?

At our early reunions Howard and Buzzie would retrieve all of us kids from whatever relatives we were living with at the time, eventually there would be five children, and we would head off on a new adventure. Howard was so handsome. He was tall, with very broad shoulders, those dark brown eyes and the nicest shaped nose. Its funny to think about his nose but it was almost perfect. This handsome curser and his Buzzie would pile us all in some run down car and we would be ecstatically happy. Howard had some favorite songs and we would sing them all, on our way to a new home. He would start off:

> "I got an old slouch hat" and we would
> join in
> "I got a roll on my shoulder
> I'm as free as a breeze and
> I'll do as I please just a bumming
> around"

Buzzie and Howards Wedding

Sometimes we would get creative and when Howard sang:

"I got an old slouch hat" we would sing
"You're just the slouch that can wear it"

Oh how we all laughed. We must have sang some songs hundreds of times.

"Oh, it ain't gonna rain no more, no more.
It ain't gonna rain no more.
How in the heck can I wash my neck
If it ain't gonna rain no more."

The verses to that one were mostly X-rated but he loved them and we sang them at the top of our happy little voices.

"Tom cat sittin' on a sewing machine
Sewing machine was fast
Took nine stitches up his tail
and one right up his a--.
Oh, it ain't gonna rain no more, no more.
It ain't gonna rain no more.
How in the heck can I wash my neck
If it ain't gonna rain no more."

In years to come I would relive those happy times over and over. I also sorted through the dozens of censored verses and would come up with five or six that could be shared with my own children.

"Black and white animal out in the woods,

Isn't that little cat pretty.
Went over there to pick it up,
But, it wasn't that kind of a kitty.
Oh, it ain't gonna rain no more, no more.
It ain't gonna rain no more
How in the heck can I wash my neck
If it ain't gonna rain no more."

The new beginnings would be filled with happiness and hope that, this time it would be forever. New beginnings were also hard work. The houses they would find were by all means sub-standard even for those early post war days, but Buzzie was a pure artist when it came to making them homey. If there were only 2x4's on the walls, we would get any scrap of wood we could beg, borrow or steal to nail up for walls. She would make paste of boiled water and flour and we would wet down layers of newspaper and apply to the walls. Sometimes we would even have real paper on top of the newspaper.

The outhouse would be scrubbed, sometimes moved to a new place. So Howard and Punky would dig a new hole and move it. I wonder now if many of those places were abandoned because the outhouse holes just got filled up--I don't know!

Buzzie could sew anything. In no time at all we would have curtains on the windows. Everything came in cloth bags then; flour, sugar, corn meal and feed for the animals. It wasn't just our family that hunted through the bags to find several with the same material. Every one we knew did it. Cloth was a precious commodity and Buzzie would exchange bags with other women or she would sew something for them in exchange for material.

She was so talented. How proud I would be of a new dress she would make me. She would ask my opinions about them beforehand. She would say things like "And do you want it to tie around the waist honey" or "do you want a little ribbon at the neck" and sure enough when she had gathered enough cloth, she would make a dress, just like I had pictured it in my mind. Did she really let me design those little dresses that are in my memories or did she feed me questions that she already had formulated answers to in her mind? I don't know and it doesn't matter. I only know it was proof that Buzzie loved me and I felt like a fairy tale princess, as she would help me into a beautiful ruffled dress. I would watch the younger children for hours, cook and clean and do anything she wanted just to give her time to treadle that old sewing machine.

People who knew Buzzie then and know me now say she would be very proud of me because I love to sew.

It is a big source of joy and accomplishment to me. And there are many time as I sit before my machine that I think lovingly and longingly about her, I wish I could tell her how much those intimate moments meant to me. I don't think I ever did!

As handsome as Howard was he didn't choose a pretty woman to marry. Buzzie was just plain. She was about 5'4" tall and as long as I knew her she was overweight. Her figure was definitely not voluptuous, but rather straight. She had chestnut brown hair and her eyes were as dark as Howards. Her complexion was olive tinted and sagged early in life. The jowl sagging may have been related to tooth loss, since as far back as I can remember Buzzie had false teeth, so did Howard. The dentist was an unknown to our kind of people unless you had your teeth all pulled and STORE BOUGHT ones replaced them. Most of our older relatives did not have teeth at all. Ida and TJ ate everything we did but they did not have a tooth in their mouth.

My first visit to the dentist occurred when I was thirteen or fourteen years old. I remember it vividly. I had eaten a banana on the bus ride home from school when the pain started. How angry I was at myself for eating that banana. No amount of rinsing with salt water or oil of clove packed into the rotten hole would relieve the pain so the following morning an aunt took me for my first tooth extraction. Did he say the roots are dying or the nerves are dying? At any rate he pulled several teeth and gave me my first introduction to oral hygiene. A toothbrush! Was that really the first time I ever had one? Heaven, help me, I don't remember. Buzzie used to tell us to scrub our teeth with a wash cloth (washrag she called it).

I always suspected Punky didn't mind her because his teeth had green edges up at the gum line.

I always obeyed Buzzie because I really wanted her to love me and not run away from us anymore. I wished Punky would have listened to her and obeyed her more too.

Punky apparently didn't listen or at least obey Buzzie about scrubbing his body either. He always had dirty nails and rough, dry patches on his elbows. I can hear Buzzie saying, "you have German

Howard Buzzies 3 kids in the
streets of Antigo, 1943 or 44

The mysterious grandpa Webster (Buzzies Dad)

Howard's service photo

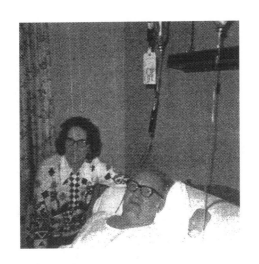

Howard's last days

Sixteen & married

Ida & TJ's Home

Baby Sqeeck

Rust". Next thing you know we would be loading up milk cans onto a wooden wagon. The horses would be hitched up to it and we would head to the lake. Punky and I would fill the cans and bring them home. Buzzie would use kettles to heat some water on the cook stove and pour it into a round washtub. Thus would start the bathing process. The exact pecking order is lost in my memory somewhere, although I believe the youngest sister went first, but I remember Punky had to bathe after all us girls were done, by this time he had three sisters, but he had "German Rust" so he bathed after we were done.

The trek to the lake as I remember occurred two or three times a week. Everything was done with water from the lake. The laundry, cleaning, bathing and animals all existed because of that water. The water for cooking and drinking was carried from a relatives house who had a well. It wasn't always the same relative since no on wanted a constant drain on their well, Howard would take the drinking water cans with us whenever we went visiting and ask if he could fill the g-- d--- things by them. Again a double hurt, the swearing and the begging people for water. You could tell that they didn't want to let us use their wells. The relative or friend would tell Howard to fill his cans this time but he really needed to get his own well.

There was one house we lived where we did have our own well. Oh we still trekked the lake water for most things but we had our own pump for drinking water. It was close to the house and had a wooden platform built over the well pit. You could look between the wooden slats and see water far below them. Most of the time! Sometimes the water was so low you couldn't see any deep down in the hole and no amount of priming the pump would make it bring up any new water. And they would fight. You see the fresh water, the drinking can, was never supposed to get empty. A certain amount was always necessary to prime the pump. When the pump was not responding and bringing up good water, Howard would keep on pumping and priming like a mad man. He would cuss and prime and cuss and pump until the reserve of drinking water was gone. Then he would use the lake water for priming. For some reason this infuriated Buzzie, something about contamination. These fights about the pump could end up with one or the other, or both of them to leave for a couple of days.

It soon became a silent promise of mine, to myself, to keep that fresh water can filled. That was one thing I could do to keep them from fighting and maybe stay by us kids more. It was a constant vigil for me. Several times a day I would be looking in the drinking water can to make sure the level of water was up.

One time while I was pumping and priming that old pump I pushed the long handle down with my right arm and split my left index finger. I had my finger under the upper handle and didn't realize it was that close to the mashing point. Now from midway up the nail to the tip of my finger, it was two pieces. How a ten year old girl withstood that pain and took care of that wound, I don't know. I don't think I ever told them! The promise to myself to keep them from fighting about that pump was not taken lightly. I honestly believed that if they knew about my finger the two of them would have fought really bad and for sure one of them would have left. The finger healed! It looks funny, the nail is curled and gets cold and numb but it works.

The place where we had a pump must have been home to us for several years. Never before or never again did Howard and Buzzie live in a house so long. Us kids always referred to it as "The Farm" and in a way it was. We had a team of horses, a pet pig, some chickens and at one time seven cows.

Oh yes, and Punky had a dog. Where the dog came from and what its' ancestry was, are unknown to me. His name was Heinz, which later in life I learned meant 57 varieties. He was a good dog and a friend to Punky, remember he only had younger sisters. Heinz would go out with my brother and me every morning and evening to get the cows. We never knew exactly where they were going to be, but Heinz would find them, he would start running and barking, and soon the dumb ole cows would start home.

Sometimes Howard would help my brother and me milk them, quite often though it was just Punky and myself. It wasn't that I didn't like the cows because I did. Each one of us kids claimed one as our personal pet. Mine was Molly and she was pregnant when we got her, I think. At least it didn't seem like a very long time after we got her that one morning Punky, Heinz and I found her out in a field with not one, but two calves. The steam was rising off them. It was so thrilling, my first experience at motherhood. Promptly named, Jack and Jill, the calves were healthy and grew fast. I took good care of them and they greeted me every day after school, for a while.

One day after school they weren't there and Buzzie told me they had been butchered. That was almost too much to bear. Howard was a killer, in my ignorant young mind. That was exactly what he had done to Porker, the pet pig.

Porker had been just one too many from a relatives sow. Pigs could only nurse so many little ones at a time, and Porker, apparently, was too slow, because there was no nipple left for him. He had been given to us before we even moved to the farm. I remember us kids tying ribbons around his neck. We would bathe him sometimes so Buzzie would let him in the house. If you scratched Porkers back he would lie down and roll over to have his stomach scratched. They used that trick to aid in butchering him.

Buzzie made us girls all stay in the house that night, just Howard and Punky went out to milk. She made a big deal of putting rag curls in our hair. Soon I knew the real reason for the night off from chores. Porker's death curdling screams permeated the kitchen. They had killed our pet! That scene, those piercing squeals, linger much fresher, in my mind than most things of that age and time. It is still a rarity to have Pork at our house and never do I cook it without thinking about Porker.

In Howard's defense it was not easy to try to make a living at farming. Us kids made a pet out of everything. If a chicken laid an egg we thought it should be a baby chick and for myself I wouldn't volunteer information about a nest of eggs somewhere. You remember I told you it was kind of like a farm. There weren't special places for animals, no chicken houses or sheep pens. There was just that one little lean-to barn where we milked and the milk house that was eventually built around the pump.

We tried to make some boundary fence lines but they were pretty feeble. Some places we piled rocks up, here and there we strung barbed wire or hammered together poplar trees to resemble fences. Those fence lines almost caused the death of my Molly.

One morning while Heinz, Punky and myself were bringing the cows in to milk we had to walk them across a fence line where big rocks were piled. Molly's hooves got caught between some rocks and she panicked and bolted into the barbed wire, tearing a long jagged cut on her udder. It was horrible and I was filled with hate myself, and hurting for her. The poor animal still had to be milked and it hurt her so much. The only treatment, I remember, was rubbing Bag Balm on her morning and night. It took a long time but her udder did heal.

I wonder if we were able to use her milk for sale at that time? I can't remember! It seems we were always having trouble with bacteria in our milk. Many times the big trucks would stop by to pick up milk and instead they would leave a tag on our milk cans.

At those times we tried to use it up. The animals all got milk, we would make butter and whipped cream. Buzzie would have little white bags hanging on the clothesline. Cottage cheese. Then everything concerning milk got scrubbed really good. The milk house, barrels, pails, cows udders and our hands, even the pump would get scrubbed down. Then the big truck would pick up our milk again. This was very important to Howard and Buzzie because it was a check coming in. Much of the time it was the only money coming in and we all looked forward to the days when the milk check came.

Sometimes we all went to town, when we got a Milk Check. There were always other relatives there too and the kids all played out in the parking lot behind the row of stores. We might even get to go into the stores on occasions. Buzzie would ask me to help her pick out some flour or feed sacks that would match ones we had at home. She made me feel very important when she said I had a good memory and could remember which bags were the same as some we already had at home. She counted on me to pick out more of the same kind.

Those were good times. We knew when they were done shopping and visiting we would stop for ice cream. The cones were hanging on the wall at the locker plant and the ice cream was in a freezer. The man would remove the paper from the cylindrical shaped ice cream, put it in the cone and hand one to each of us kids. I don't know if Howard had to buy the ice cream or if it was a customer gratuity. I just knew it was always the last stop in town and the best part of the trip.

You see people like us didn't have refrigeration since we didn't have electricity. So we rented space at a locker plant in town. The butchered animals were always kept in the locker plant and we would go get our meat there. All our meat except the venison. That meat, Howard and Buzzie would cook and can in mason jars. Apparently they didn't want anyone to know they killed deer. I used to hear the word Poacher used and I believe it because years later Howard would spend a night in jail for shooting a deer out of season. But in those days, I just thought it was just the way venison was prepared. It was just a given thing; pork, beef, sheep and chickens were carried to town to be stored in the locker plant and venison was canned and stored in someone's cellar. It was a good thing we had our own cellar on the farm because when Howard and Buzzie were both gone at the same time it gave us kids something to eat.

There were so many good times on the farm. Buzzie was a good housekeeper and somehow she made it enjoyable for us to help her. Days off from school would find us all at jobs. The washtubs would be filled with hot water for washing the clothes this day. Sometimes she had a washing machine but many times Buzzie would be scrubbing on a washboard in the tubs, one with hot water and big bars of brown soap, she called Fels Naptha and another tub with cold water to rinse the suds out of the hot clothes. We would scrub the floors and polish the furniture with Old English polish so that you could hardly see all the scratches and holes. We would fill the lamps with kerosene and wash the glass shades, the shades got black real fast but on cleaning days they were sparkling.

When the housework was all done Buzzie would make us great food. One of our favorites was dough gobs. She would pull off pieces of her partially risen bread dough and fry them in hot lard and then roll them in sugar. They were so good! Sometimes we would all sit around the big cook-stove and she would tell great stories. It wasn't until many years later I would learn that Buzzie was a pathological liar. She didn't know herself which stories were true because she had told so many, so often. But back there with the family I believed every word she uttered.

Buzzie said her parents were wealthy and raised her a strict Catholic girl. She could trace her family tree back to the Mayflower. Her family came from England and Ireland but more recently from Iowa. Her grandfather had discovered that strawberries and tomatoes were edible, before that nobody had been brave enough to try eating them. Her relatives had written the first dictionary. (Well, her maiden name was Webster). She had won a debate in high school, proving a horse pushed a wagon instead of pulling it and now it would be written in all school textbooks forever, because of her. The famous people she had met and all the wonderful places she had been and we were spellbound. I sure was lucky to have such a smart, talented mother!

But wait, she was talented. She could make a meal out of vegetable blossoms, almost any kind. It seems we were always hungry and many times couldn't wait for the garden to ripen, so we would pick the biggest blossoms, pumpkin was very good, dip them in egg and flour and fry them in (what else) lard. I'm telling you they were good. She made dandelion greens seem like a rare treat. If we didn't have butter (sometimes we had to send all the creme in so our milk check would be bigger) she would make us lard sandwiches with salt and pepper on it. And her radish sandwiches were delicious. It seemed like radishes got ripe before most other things in the garden so Buzzie would slice them real thin and make us sandwiches on hot bread. We loved them.

One of her biggest talents was playing the piano. Oh the good times we would have. A kerosene lamp sitting on top of the piano and all of us standing around her, she would plunk away for hours.

I was sure no one ever had a more special mother.

But those times were soon over and she would be gone again. Sometimes Howard would say she was never coming back or he didn't want her back and I would go by myself and cry. Sometimes He would cry and ask us if we knew where she was. Sometimes he would go look for her. It's a mystery to me how she could run away because Buzzie never drove a car and in those days we were seven miles from town.

It was hard to be without either one of my parents. When Howard was gone we were really stuck. No car and no store in walking distance. But I think it was harder when Buzzie was gone. The times when they both were gone were the worst. We would try to keep things up, especially our spirits, but it was hard!

When the fighting between Howard and Buzzie became more frequent us kids would know one, or both of them would soon leave us and we lived in fear each day. I remember we would get off the school bus and run to the house anxiously hoping someone would be there. The last time they left the farm, they were together. I don't know how long they were gone before a relative came for us, but I do remember we kept up a semblance of family life for a while. We went to school, did the chores and ran home every day hoping they, or at least one of them had returned., I could bake bread and make some food but soon the cellar was empty. We were down to eating canned cherry sandwiches and dill pickles. I would tell the siblings to eat their lunch away from sight of other kids so we wouldn't be poked fun of. Other people didn't have to know that we were alone. I was afraid if other people saw how little we carried in our lunch, they would know that we were parentless. Somehow in those early days I equated that into being us kids' fault. Also it made me ashamed for other people to know what our parents were really like because so many of our friends thought they were special. Our parents did not boss us around like some of the other kids parents did. We got to come and go pretty much as we wanted. I don't think we ever had a curfew! So our friends thought we were lucky.

Ida and TJ's house was about two miles away from the farm and just a short way from their house was their youngest daughter and son-in-law. It was this young Aunt and her husband who took us in. I was ten years old when we started living with Aunt Dory. One day, she just showed up at the farm and said we were going home with her and stay a while. She helped us pack a few things and off we went to live with her and her husband in their little tar paper shack. Heinz stayed at the farm.

It was just a few years ago I asked Aunt Dory how she knew we were alone. To their credit Howard and Buzzie had written her a letter and asked her to take us in. There simply wasn't any room at Ida and TJ's house at that time because they were raising five children from one of their daughters.

It wasn't a bad year at Aunt Dorys. Oh, it was very crowded but she was always there for us. Us three girls had a bed over in one corner and she hung a blanket or curtain in front of it so we had privacy. I remember one time she told us Howard and Buzzie were coming up for a visit. They had made this new start in the big city of Milwaukee and things were going good. Both of them had jobs and as soon as "they got on their feet" they were coming to get us kids. Something must have happened because the visit didn't materialize. Perhaps they hadn't gotten to their feet yet!

For consolation Aunt Dory took us all into town to see a movie. I don't remember the name of the movie but it was awesome. The picture was in color, just like real life. And it was inside a big building, with cushioned seats for everyone to sit on. We had seen movies before but they were outside. Some men would set up a screen that resembled a window shade and back a ways from that was a gadget on three legs that would shine a light on the screen. Neighbor children, cousins and us kids would sit on the ground and watch this black and white magic light, show us adventures of "Hopalong Cassidy". At the end of each show he would be close to death, perilously perched on a cliff sitting on his horse Topper or surrounded by bad guys with pistols pointed at him. We would walk home wondering how Hopalong would escape but we would have to wait until the next week or month (I'm not sure of the time in between) until the magic machine came back. The movie Aunt Dory took us to told the whole story right then and there. It was a glorious adventure. I'm sure we would rather have had the visit from Howard and Buzzie, but Aunt Dory tried.

There weren't any children of their own at Dory's and Lymans house. I think she hadn't been married very long. Many years later they started to have children of their own and ended up with seven sons.

While we lived with her we got introduced to bible study. Some traveling preacher would come to Ida and TJ's house and would talk to the cousins and us about sin and evil. The relatives would sit in the kitchen talking about the sin and evil of Howard and Buzzie. On those nights TJ joined the kitchen group or went to his bedroom. I really liked the bible stories but I wished I couldn't hear the kitchen conversations.

How could they be saying such awful things about handsome Howard and talented Buzzie, but they always did. TJ's favorite line was "those kids weren't raised, they just grew, like weeds". I believe he was responsible for the bible study lessons. What did they call Buzzie, "A Harlot"? I didn't know what that was but the tone of their voices let me know it wasn't a compliment. Sometimes I could hear Aunt Dory defending them. She claimed they must have done something right as parents or else how could I be such a good girl. TJ would say, like always, "some people are born good". I don't think I ever wanted to be "born good", I just wanted to be back on the farm. I only wanted to be with my Howard and Buzzie.

Now, that we lived at Aunt Dory's house we started school in September with all of our cousins and neighboring children. When we had been on the farm we didn't go to school until potato- picking season was over. Antigo was known (still is) for its potato farms.

Well Howard, Buzzie, Punky and myself would be out in the fields very early. There were sometimes we had to take my two sisters with us to the fields but that slowed down the picking so we tried to leave them by some relative. We would crawl along picking up potatoes until we filled a gunny sack (100 pounds) full, then put a little number card on top of the sack.

At the end of the day the boss would count all of our little cards and pay us a dime a- piece.

The season only lasted a few weeks. Then Howard and Buzzie would buy us all shoes and we would go to school. People like us didn't wear shoes in the summer. But that year by Aunt Dory's we went to school in September when it started. Every day on the bus we passed by our farm, it made me so lonesome. Soon the fields grew up and it was plain to see no one lived there.

I don't know what happened to all the furniture or even the animals from the farm. Did the relatives sell them or divide them up – I don't know. After a while even Heinz came to live with us at Aunt Dory's. Because he had turned out to be some kind of miracle dog. Everyone said dogs didn't live with the sickness Heinz had suffered one winter. He got very weak, threw up a lot and had white drool at his mouth. Punky would not be talked into having him killed. He fought, swore, cried and begged for Heinz's life and in the end he got it, and nursed him back to health. Wherever you saw Punky you saw Heinz. Aunt Dory would play cards with us girls sometimes but Punky and Heinz were always off exploring. I suspect they took a lot of walks back to the old farm.

The following year Howard and Buzzie came and got us kids. It was time for school to start and they had rented a nice place for all of us. They made it sound grand and we were a happy family again. Off we went to a new beginning. Singing at the top of our happy little voices and loving our handsome and talented parents for coming to get us.

The first place we lived was right by a lake and somehow we had access to a boat. Maybe it was someone's summer retreat and we had permission to use it in the fall. We didn't live there long. That first year we would move several times. The cabin on the lake, the back of a vacant store, an upstairs apartment in the big city of Milwaukee and back out close to the first cabin only into a big house. There were some good times there. Us kids could walk to the lake and swim. We were still dealing with an outhouse, but there was water in the house and electric lights.

It was at this big house I learned Buzzie was having another baby. There was a big screened in porch on the front of that ole house and Buzzie and I spent long hours sitting together and sewing for the new baby to come soon. We embroidered little animal squares and sewed them all together for a quilt. We hemmed dozens of squares of white flannel for diapers and with colored flannel we made little gowns and sacques. It was a bonding time for two women and I was happy.

We had spent the school hiatus back up north that summer hopping from one relative to another but mostly by Ida and TJ's, those five children they had been raising had gone to live with their own father now and so Ida and TJ had room for us girls. Punky had been sent to spend the summer with an uncle who had a big farm. The uncle had a reputation for being a hard worker and a strict disciplinarian. Why Punky needed this I didn't know, but Buzzie and Howard said he did.

For me it was a year of surprises. Grandma Ida had scolded Buzzie right away for how I looked in a tee shirt. One of the first things she bought me was a brassiere. It must have been necessary because I would wear that same size for twenty years.

Then don't you know while I was spending some weeks with one of Ida's daughter (a favorite aunt of mine) and the one, relatives said I looked like, I had an accident. While riding a boys bike my foot slipped off the peddle and I hit the bar hard between my legs. The next day I explained this to my aunt and told her of the bleeding. Surprise! She went on to explain about a cycle of womanhood and how every 28 days this would happen to me. No. Not the slipping off the bike, only the bleeding part. What a thing to happen and she was so shocked that I didn't know anything about such goings on. Oh dear, more reasons for relatives to talk bad about my talented Buzzie.

I had heard that word menstruation some years earlier. A neighbor girl's mother at the farm had bragged about her daughter starting her menstruation and at the time I just figured it was a special thing and people like us didn't get it, whatever it was, I never asked. Now here was my aunt saying I had it. She gave me a little elastic belt with hooks on the front and back and some store bought cotton pads to wear between my legs. She explained about changing the pads and keeping real clean or I would smell bad and everyone would know. I began to have my doubts about this menstruation business being such a great thing and I hoped Buzzie wouldn't go bragging about me.

When we went back home for school that year, I told Buzzie all that had happened to me during the summer. She told me how people like us didn't use store bought pads and gave me my own supply of torn white flour sacks. This pile was hers and this pile was mine. They were to be soaked in "Hi Lex" (a bottled bleach) water until I was done bleeding each month and then scrubbed and hung up to dry, careful always to be discreet and replace them in the same spot. She also said I was a woman now and so we bonded that summer before I turned twelve. Mother and daughter sharing the secrets of womanhood and preparing for the birth of young Howard.

That was to be our new brother's name and what he was always called. For his early years anyway. In adulthood he picked up the horrible name of Lurch. I believe because he grew so huge. He, like myself never had a nickname in the family days.

Oh Buzzie called me Sherry because that is what her father was known by, That wonderful, almost mystical person from her life that I had no recollection of. She said she named me after her parents and it was a special name. He, the mysterious grandfather was "Sheridon Philip Webster" and his wife was "Nora Dean". Nora Dean and her oldest daughter were the ones I lived with when I was very young and the ones who read the bible to me. Therefore I became Sharon Nora. I don't remember the other three siblings ever called or referred to by their given name.

The sister next to me, although she was given the birth name of Dorothy, was always "Mocky" and the baby sister was "Squeak". So these were the children of Howard and Buzzie. Punky was almost fourteen when Randy was born, Mocky was nine, Squeak was six and I was almost twelve.

While waiting for the birth of young Howard, Buzzie hadn't left us for any length of time but Howard had and the serious fighting was on again. She screamed a lot about a "Madaline" and he screamed about lots of men, many of them uncles. He claimed she was trying to drive him crazy like her mother had driven her father to the "Nut House". She cried and screamed back that her father had been in an accident and had a steel plate in his head.

Oh my word, was that mysterious grandfather that I was named after really crazy before he died, I was afraid to ask. What could I remember about Sheridon Philip--? Nothing! I have a photograph of him and I heard stories of him chasing Punky with an ax, but I can't remember him.

His house is hazy in my mind too. It was big and had a large tree in the front yard. That tree. I remember something about that tree! Punky was trying to raise a swing higher off the ground one day because our feet dragged when we swung on it. He tied a big knot in the rope and put a ham bone in the knot to hold it in place. Then the swing was too high to climb onto. My job was to hold a stool there so he could reach the swing. When he swung back I was to pull the stool away. I must have been too slow because on the backswing he kicked me between the eyes and knocked me out. I don't remember it but I do have an inch long scar between my eyes. That is all I can remember of life at that mysterious grandfather's place. I was three when they told me my namesake had died.

Now here were Howard and Buzzie saying these horrible things about Sheridon Philip. That wasn't the only thing they were fighting about though and I knew the end was close again. Once more on the bus ride home from school I would pray that they be there and whenever I would be babysitting for someone else I would insist on going back home just in case. Before the fighting I would spend the night and catch the school bus from the babysitting job. Now I wanted to sleep at home in case Buzzie and Howard were not there. If Howard and Buzzie were not around Punky could be very mean to the other siblings. I could keep him in line and be a buffer for the other kids. It hadn't taken too many wrestling matches for him to realize I could hurt him back and so he was better behaved when I was around. Mocky had not learned to cook yet and Punky would only cook for himself. So I felt a responsibility to be there for the little ones

Of course it happened, one day neither parent came home. I don't know how long they were gone but to their credit they eventually called a neighbor of ours. The message was "to be at this neighbors house at a specified time and wait for a phone call".

This neighbor was within walking distance and I had babysat for her on several occasions. She was a gracious Lady and always paid me promptly, the going rate of twenty-five cents an hour. The family was all nice and I figured they must have been rich because they had a telephone and two cars. As long as I had to wait at her house for the telephone call, the Lady would run some errands and I could baby-sit. This was a good plan.

The folks did call and I believe it was the first time I ever talked on the telephone. It sure seemed strange to hear Howard talking quietly to me and yet I couldn't see him. What was he saying?--- Good news. Him and Buzzie were together again and soon they would come for us kids. He said to start packing too. But not to let anyone know that they weren't home or that we would be moving. With some encouraging words about us all being together soon and a last admonishment about telling no one, he said goodbye.

I was anxious to get back to our house and tell my siblings about the good news but the neighbor lady was gone a long time. When she did return she was in a visiting mood. Usually I liked her talking to me but this particular day I was in a hurry. I told her I needed to go make supper because my folks would be a little late. "Oh and what are you making tonight" she asked. What it was I don't remember but what she said she was having sure sounded strange.

Rich folks must eat differently I thought, because she said she was eating crow, this night. Crow? Punky used to bring me little birds and tiny bird eggs to cook and I never liked them and would not eat them. Now here was this lovely lady talking about eating crow. I didn't dwell on the thought too long because I was running home to tell my siblings about a new beginning. Oh it ain't gonna rain no more, no more.

The new beginning this time was smack dab in the big city of Milwaukee. The folks had been working in this big city all along and they had lived here several times. In fact once when they had just Punky and me we had lived there with them. I must have been very young at that time because there were slats on the side of my bed.

My only real memory of Milwaukee was of Howard screaming and chasing some animal with a broom in the middle of the night. He was very upset because this animal was up in the crib with me. Howard turned on all the lights and no one slept any more that night. The next day Punky and I were taken up to our maternal grandparents. Rats, they told our grandparents. Now we were going to live in that big city again. Guess they figured we were big enough to fight off the rats by ourselves now or maybe they didn't live there anymore. I didn't know.

Our first apartment was upstairs, another family lived upstairs too but there was a door between us and their place. Downstairs was a family with a lot of kids and would you believe, they all had German Rust. That was really strange to me because this big city apartment building had water inside. All you had to do was turn a handle and water came running out into a big white bowl that Howard and Buzzie called a Zink. It would be some time before I learned it was a sink or lavatory. There was another big white bowl sitting on the floor with a handle to turn on, and water came rushing into it. The water just splashed around for a minute and then ran right out the bottom of the big bowl. This modern contraption was where we went to the bathroom. Maybe we were rich now like the lady I had babysat for. They had a room like that too. I wondered if we would start eating crow.

There were sure wonders to explore in this new place, but some of them were a little frightening. Especially outside of the building. There were no trees and instead of grass there was hard stuff everywhere. Some of the hard stuff was black and some of it was grey but all of it hurt if you fell on it.

Right outside our windows ran these noisy big buses. They were much different than our old school buses and they ran all day and all night long. These buses hung from a heavy wire on their roofs and there were knots in the wire, whenever they would hit a knot they made loud clanging noises. When the buses stopped to let people on or off, there *were* loud hissing noises and clanging metal noises. It was very hard to sleep in the big city apartment with those noisy buses right outside our window. Buzzie called them streetcars but they were much bigger than cars, in fact they were much bigger than any bus I had ever seen.

Every new beginning of course meant a new school and I was used to it. Never could I have been prepared for this newest school. I was in seventh or eighth grade and in the city that meant I couldn't go with my brother and sisters anymore.

This big building was called a Junior High School. It had lots of rooms and just as many teachers. My schooling so far had been in little buildings with two or three teachers. Some schools had two rooms with the smaller kids, grades one to four in one room and the fifth to eighth graders in another. One teacher would also be the principal. Well, now I was told to move around from room to room. I soon learned to listen for the bell because that meant to pack up your books and go to another room. Why there was even a room where you didn't study anything. You just went there to listen for the bell to ring so you could start going to the other rooms for lessons. It was so hard to understand.

My siblings were walking to a smaller school just a few blocks from the apartment. Not Punky. He was still within walking distance of school, but it was a High School.

My school was too far from the apartment to walk. The worst part of all! I was to ride that scary streetcar most of the way to school. The first time the big streetcar stopped and I attempted to climb up the metal steps to get inside my right leg hit the top metal step and started to bleed. I must have been quite a sight, a strangely dressed kid with wild long hair and dried blood running down her leg and this was my first day at the new school.

There were a few blocks leaving the school building where there weren't any wires or knots for the streetcars to run on. Everyday I would walk those few blocks and wonder if I could/ or world climb back up on the streetcar for the ride home. Many times I would walk all the way home. It got to be a game with myself. If I walked I could take the money (I think it was seven cents) and buy a frozen Milky Way candy bar. I would take the tiniest little bites and see how long I could make the chocolate taste last in my mouth. Some days the back of my feet hurt too bad and I would succumb to climbing aboard the metal monster.

My heels always had blisters on them it seemed, they would bleed often and I put pieces of my writing tablets around them to keep the blood contained. People like us didn't have socks and I suspect Howard and Buzzie didn't know exactly what size shoes to buy us---I don't know. Just one time I remember my parents being concerned about my bleeding heels. There was a red streak running up the leg when I got home. I don't remember it hurting but then it was winter and my feet were pretty numb from the snow. Both parents were nice to me that evening and Buzzie had me soak in warm salt water, she said from now on there would always be streetcar money for me. Gee, maybe I hadn't always walked out of choice.

There was a girl in that Junior High School that had been a neighbor of ours up at the farm. Her and her family only lived by the farm in the summertime. They had a house on a big hill close to the lake and we passed it on our trek for water from the lake. In the winter when the Geiger house was empty us kids would take cardboard boxes over there and slide down that big hill. It was fun and we had spent a lot of hours there. One winter the Geigers were in their house and we didn't even know it (perhaps it was Christmas vacation). Instead of being mad at us kids Mrs. Geiger invited us in for hot cocoa. She was sure a nice lady! Now here was her daughter at my Junior High School. She talked to me that first day but never again. After that first day she would look away if our eyes met and she just acted like I wasn't there, if her and other girls were talking. I guess she was citified (that is what people like us referred to people who were used to city ways).

Sometimes I would hear her and her girlfriends talking in the bathrooms while they smoked their cigarettes. The conversations were about boys and what they did to them or with them. I could not have joined in with those girls even if they had wanted me too. I was in awe of them though with their colored nails and lips. They all had skinny eyebrows just like Buzzie and I thought they were so glamorous. Sometimes I would sit in the little toilet cubicle long after I had finished using it, just to hear them talk more.

There was one girl who Befriended me in Junior High School. Her name was Sandy and she was within walking distance from school. Many days I would walk home with Sandy before heading home myself. She didn't like to go home alone because both of her parents worked and it was quiet and lonely in her big house. Sandy did not have a single brother or sister. She was really alone. She had wonderful food at her house though and we always ate plenty. There was candy in dishes and ice cream in her refrigerator. She didn't even ask anyone if she could eat things, we just did it. Sandy was the only friend I can remember making in that first year in the big city.

One afternoon Sandy and I went to a movie. Soon two teenage boys sat beside us. I whispered to Sandy we should go out to the lobby and once we got there I told her my story of the last movie I had been to. It had happened a year or two before this one. I knew that because we still lived out by the rich lady who ate crow.

A girl from school and myself had taken a bus into town. This girl was from Poland and she was so brave. There was nothing she would not try and she was great fun. Her real name was Hania But everyone called her Anna, except me, I liked the Polish way of saying her name. Like I said Hania was a very adventurous person and somehow arranged this big undertaking of the bus ride, movie and a trip to a hamburger place for the two of us. Well just like this movie place, as soon as the lights turned out some guy came and sat beside me. It made me very nervous so Hania and I had got up and sat in different seats. When the movie was over and we were heading for the hamburger place we discovered my money was gone. The guy in the movie had stolen my whole three dollars. That was weeks of babysitting money. I know I cried and was afraid for a long time. Now here were two guys sitting beside us in a movie again. I was afraid it was happening all over again.

Sandy called me a sissy and said she would hold my money but she was sure the guys wanted to neck with us. What? Yes, she was sure the boys wanted to kiss us. Sandy was right! We didn't go back to the very same movie seats but close enough so the two boys could see us and sure enough they came and sat by us again. Soon this boy put his arm around my shoulder and then he kissed me. My first kiss by anyone outside of a relative.

Him and the other boy went out to the lobby, to smoke I believe, because he smelled like cigarettes. That's the way the whole movie went. Whenever the boys went out to the lobby I would borrow Sandy's lipstick and put more on, more kissing, more trips to the lobby and more lipstick. We had never seen those boys before and never saw them again. I was feeling pretty grown up and smart on the walk home, those boys and all that kissing were all Sandy and I talked about.

Howard started screaming and swearing as soon as we walked in the door. Sandy left for home in a hurry. Buzzie was just laughing hysterically at me. What in the world was going on? Howard continued cursing and threatening all sorts of things would happen to me if I ever came home looking like that again. He finally left the apartment with a loud slam of the door. Why is he so mad at me I questioned Buzzie? She told me to go look in the bathroom mirror. I did look ridiculous! There was red lipstick smeared all over face and chin. I still wasn't sure why it had made Howard so mad though. Buzzie said he just didn't like to think his little girl was growing up. Oh! So it was a grown up kind of thing. I had thought so and now Buzzie had confirmed it.

Soon after the movie incident we moved from the apartment. This time the move wasn't by choice. A teacher in the Junior High School had the newspaper in class one day and she was showing us pictures of this filthy building and explaining why the city would tear it down. She was saying the plumbing was not functioning and it was over run with rats. The word she used was, Condemned. Then the teacher asked if any of us had ever seen the building? I told her I lived there! She seemed upset about the whole thing now. I told her I had never seen any rats there, and in my mind I was wondering if rats didn't know how to climb stairs.

Anyway it was hard to understand why the city would tear down that building. It was nicer than most places we had ever lived and Buzzie always kept our apartment clean. If the toilet wouldn't flush on its own we would just pour a bucket of water in it and it would go down, much better conditions than an outhouse. They did tear it down! When I got home from school that day everyone was in a panic. There were big signs nailed to the building with the words CONDEMNED printed on them. No one could habitat the building after such and such date. Time to move!

Our next house was close enough we didn't even change schools. It was a real house too and no one but our family lived there. There was some grass in back of it and one big tree that grew Indian Cigars on it. We were so lucky! Howard was working at an Appliance store now delivering new refrigerators and freezers to people. We seemed to have money now and store bought clothes. Oh Buzzie still sewed some but I remember she took me shopping for clothes because I was going to start regular High School. We picked out a corduroy jacket and skirt, some blouses and shoes that I got to try on and make sure they fit. Life was good!

My first day of High School and I was all dressed up in my corduroy clothes. Buzzie was telling me never to call my brother Punky again. She said he had a given name and I was to use it. That was going to be hard because no one had ever called him anything but Punky in all my life. I told her I would not forget. He, Ray, that was his brand new name, was going to show me the way to school. He said I couldn't walk to close to him. For some reason unclear to me, we were both in the ninth grade. Ray must have gone there the year before since he knew the way and also some of the other kids. But Buzzie always told people it was because I was so smart in school and they had skipped me up a grade. I was still in my Ostrich days and believed everything she said so apparently I didn't remember, or know, what year or years the school people had skipped me. Anyway Punky was almost fifteen and I was almost thirteen when we left for High School. Me at least half a block behind him and if I closed the gap between us more than that he would turn around and yell at me. He didn't seem to like me much!

So much happened that year of High School that it is hard for me to remember the correct order of events. There was the usual amount of moving from house to house but for some reason we stayed in the same school. It was the same School District my parents would say. After the house with the Indian Cigar tree we lived in an apartment again.

There was a Spanish speaking family upstairs from us. I remember the littlest boy wore white stockings on his legs and arms. He had Excema they said and I knew about Eczema because Buzzie used to have it when we lived on the farm. Her hands would crack and bleed. They had raw places and scabs on them often. It was very painful for her and here was this little boy with Excema all over him. Poor little thing. I would babysit him sometimes and have to put salve on his raw places. He didn't cry much.

The Spanish lady would make us her kind of food sometimes always with thin pancakes rolled around the food. She didn't like to do dishes, I figured, since all her food could be eaten by holding it in your hand.

Another house we lived in that year, we were upstairs and below us lived an Indian women with three or four Indian daughters and a man with blond hair, her boyfriend, Buzzie said. My parents got along well with Parnell and the Indian family and for years after we moved from that apartment they would visit each other. That was quite unusual, most times when we moved we never saw those people again but Parnell and Audrey found us no matter where we moved, Even if we moved to different cities.

The house I remember the most about that year was very big and it had a concrete front porch. We would sit on that porch for hours and watch the people and cars go by.

Whenever we would move to a new house or apartment it would have to be completely redone. I think that is how we paid the landlords for letting us live there. Howard and Buzzie would strike these deals, to paint, paper, clean and make the place look really nice in exchange for allowing us all to live there rent free. It was hard work and half the time we would be walking around wet paint and paper but the challenges and rewards after we finished were very rewarding. We would live in this nice clean pretty place until the landlord would want money. Then the process would start all over again.

While we still lived in the house with the Indian cigar Tree I must have turned into a butterfly or one of those big moths that secrete an odor because boys started smelling me. Buzzie was always bragging about it and encouraging me to go out with them.

I did go to a prom with one boy that fall. His name was Bruce and he was in eleventh grade. I guess he was nice. I know he brought me flowers to wear on my dress but there wasn't any good spot to pin them on that strapless dress. Buzzie had bought me a beautiful white dress with little pink flowers on it. The material looked like our kitchen curtains but it sure didn't feel like curtains. It was so stiff and itchy that my skin got red every place it touched me and by the end of the night I had raw places under my arms. I'm not sure if I was just shy or if I didn't feel comfortable around Bruce I just know we never got to be boyfriend and girlfriend. Bruce came over to our house a few times after the Prom but I don't remember ever going anyplace with him again. Howard didn't like Bruce, but then Howard never liked any of the boys who came to see me except for Critter.

If you went out our front door by the Indian Cigar Tree, there was an alley across the street. Two or three houses down that alley lived Critter. He was sixteen and didn't go to school anymore, instead he worked in a garage, fixing cars. He was a friend of Punky's but he mostly spent time with Howard. Critter didn't have a Dad and him and Howard were always together. I don't know which one of them could swear the most or tell more dirty stories. If we took a trip up to Ida and TJ's house Critter went with us. Howard and Critter would sit around drinking brandy, telling foul stories and laughing uproariously. The two of them would go drinking at bars, sometimes Punky would go with them, sometimes Buzzie and I would go too.

Six months earlier Howard had been so mad at me for letting that boy kiss me at the movies but now he would get mad at me if I didn't let Critter kiss me. I wonder if he knew that Critter was always trying to do more than just kiss me. I would try to avoid him but he was always there. I of Punky's and currently a friend of mine was having a Christmas party at her house. Punky and I were both invited and so was Rudy. There were a dozen or so teenagers there but Rudy claimed he only saw me. I don't remember talking to him that night. The following day our party hostess, Bonnie, told me he had been asking many things about me and wanted my phone number, was it okay if she gave it to him. It was! I think I was impressed. After all he was a senior in High School, not the same one as we attended but one far away on the north side of the city. Come to think of it I don't know why his school was so far away. His house was only a few blocks from ours. Rudy started coming over and he would take me places sometimes, a movie, a friends house, his houses and even to Church a couple of times. His hands didn't have grease under the nails and he wore slacks. I soon discovered they were always the same slacks, burnt orange color and pegged at the bottom. Rudolf or Rudy, as he liked to be called had one really bad feature, his top teeth were all brown and rotten looking. He had been kicked in the mouth while playing football he said. Well, I liked him better than Critter and when he was over Critter wouldn't stay long.

Actually Critter was coming over less and less. He no longer lived right down the alley and also Howard did not have as much time to spend with him. Howard and Buzzie were pretty busy right then. They were trying to run their own Cartage business now instead of just working for one store. They were paying several guys to help them deliver the big appliances too. Howard swore Buzzie was running around with every hired hand they ever had. They were fighting more and more these days. About the only thing they agreed on was the fact that neither of them liked Rudy hanging around so much. He was too old for me, they said and was always telling me what to do. The fights were getting pretty physical at home. Once Buzzie threw a big kettle of hot Chili at Howard. I don't think it hit him but he was crying anyway and trying to clean it up off the walls and floor. Another day I came in from school and Howard was standing in the kitchen with a knife in his chest. It really freaked me out and I could hardly dial the phone I was shaking so badly. Buzzie sounded so cruel that day. She said it was just a small knife and besides she was sure he had meant to stab her but she tore herself out of his gasp just as the knife struck so he had hit himself by accident.

They were always wanting us kids to believe their side of the story or fight, whoever was telling it. When one parent talked to you about a particular story or fight it didn't even sound like the same incident. In between, each parent would shower attention on us kids, whenever they were around. Howard would take us out drinking to the bars. He would give us money and cigarettes. As soon as Ray turned sixteen

Howard bought him a car. Buzzie bought me another formal, this time to go to a dance with Rudy for his High School graduation. She would let my girlfriends and I dress up in our formals and have private dinner parties in the dining room. We would even have fancy alcoholic drinks in champagne glasses. We were never told what to do that year. We never had a curfew like our friends and if one of my girlfriends wanted to skip school we could all just spend the day at our house. Buzzie would even write an excuse, if we could find her to write one.

This time they would divorce Buzzie said. She had papers served on Howard. He cried and cried, big tears fell on us kids as he hugged us goodbye and his nose ran on us. But he had to go! The policeman said as he stood there waiting for him. Us kids were all crying too, after he left and Buzzie got very mad at us. On and on she ranted and raved about all the horrible things Howard had done to all of us. How he had beat us kids when we were small. I actually could only remember one time Howard had hit me.

We were still on the farm when some cousins and my siblings and I all pushed the big horse wagon up a steep hill. We were instructed by Punky to hold onto the long poles, which usually were hooked up to the horses. "Hold them inside the wagon" he instructed, "I'll push to get the wagon rolling, jump in and we'll all ride down the hill". He did push and we did hold the poles and it worked just like he had said it would. A big pile of kids rolling and tumbling, laughing like crazy at the bottom of that hill. Laughing until Howard came out, cursing, screaming and pulling his belt off at the same time. We were lined up, instructed to pull our pants down or our dresses up and slapped with Howards belt. No cousin or sibling was missed, we all got spanked royally. Buzzie soothingly explained to me later that it was fear for our safety that made him hit us all so hard. She said if the wooden poles had fallen forward of the wagon and dug into the ground all of us kids could have been thrown out, head first, and maybe have gotten killed. So that whipping and the threat of another was all I could recall.

The threat might have been at about the same time. I know the same cousins were staying overnight with us at the farm. These cousins were notorious for wetting their beds at night. Before retiring that evening we were all threatened with beatings if anyone wet the bed. None of Howard and Buzzies kids had ever been bed wetters so we knew who the threats were directed at. Horror's! The next morning there was a wet spot on one of the beds and I was lying on it. Howard never said a word. Later while Buzzie and I were making the beds she told me that Howard figured one of the cousins had done it but pushed me onto it in my sleep. I don't know. Some cousin of mine may know!

On this day when the divorce papers were served, that was the only beating or threat of one that I could think of---Oh yes, the lipstick and movie business. But Buzzie was screaming about a lot of beatings he had performed on us. How cruel he had been to all of us. How he had run around on her and ran away from us so many times. "Remember Madeline" she screamed. Actually I couldn't remember that either. Oh, I remembered hearing the name some years earlier but I had never seen the mysterious woman or heard Howard talk of her. I'm sure Buzzie just wanted to harden our hearts against Howard so we wouldn't feel so sad about the policeman making him leave. I tried! I know Punky joined in and remembered many hard and hurtful things that Howard had done to him, but those were his memories. I just could not remember any terrible things about my handsome Dad.

Buzzie started staying away from the house even more now. One day she bought new suitcases and a lot of pretty clothes. She couldn't stand it any longer and would move out West. What she couldn't stand was Howard's frequent visits and also she said he spied on her and followed her everyplace she went. He had made it so rough on one of her young boyfriends that the boyfriend had moved out west by his parent's. He was to send for Buzzie as soon as he got settled. She was packed and waiting for some days when a yellow telegram finally came. It was just a few words and I can picture them still.

DUE TO CIRCUMSTANCES KID HAD
TO MOVE TO CAROLINA.-----L. MOSS

Buzzie unpacked her suitcase!

The Moss family was back in my childhood memories some place. We were living in a deserted church building at that time and the Moss family was within walking distance from us. We took the school buss to the same two room school that we later attended on the farm. The bus would drop us off by Ida and TJ's if, we asked the driver to. How we liked the days when we could go there. We would run out to the place where the kitchen table sat in that big church building and hope there would be a note telling us to get off the bus at Ida and TJ's house.

I remember one particular note. It was a little hard to read. I hadn't gotten much experience at written words yet, just printing. The note was written in Cursive Writing and I was sure it said to go by our grandparents after school. It read "We'll be home late, don't go by grandma's house". So---happy day we all piled off the school bus by Ida and TJ's house. No one was home. It wasn't too long before Howard, Buzzie, Ida and TJ all showed up. We were in big trouble for disobeying but it didn't last too long when I explained about the note. In fact Ida starting laughing real hard and soon they all laughed. I learned a lesson that day, don't meant Do Not and also just one little word can change the whole meaning of something. Just one little word!

The memories of the Moss family are stuck in this time frame. L. was the mother of the whole tribe, a big woman with very black hair. There was a girl about my age and a boy, named Kid Smith. Why Kid had a different last name I never heard, but he was a few years older than Punky. We didn't live in that church too long but we must have kept in touch because years later Kid came to work for Howard in the Cartage Business.

Kids wife was a funny looking woman. She wore thick glasses and didn't have much hair. The few times she was at our house she had a baby perched on one hip holding a bottle. I do remember Buzzie telling her one time that the baby's bottle was sour. "Oh it is not" said this funny looking little woman and she put the bottle in the baby' mouth. It looked to me like there were lumps in the baby's bottle, but he drank it!

One time Howard, Buzzie, Kid Smith and us kids were all in a car heading up north. Howard got really mad about something, pulled the car over, got out and started walking in the opposite direction. He stuck out his thumb and a car stopped and picked him up. I couldn't imagine what would happen now because Buzzie couldn't drive. A little talk in the front seat and then Kid got out but he only walked around the car and got in Howards spot, literally. We continued heading up North but we would stop now and then. Us kids were supposed to be sleeping in the car while Buzzie and Kid were inside this place getting a drink. I couldn't sleep and it seemed like hours since I had seen anyone. With all the nerve and/ or courage I could muster up I finally walked in that place. Somehow I had to know if Buzzie had left us too. We sure couldn't live in that car! And I would have to make some plans if she were gone too. I opened that bar door ever so slowly and there she was. She did not yell or anything. In fact she told me to sit next to her and bought me a drink. She put her arms around Kid and asked me what I thought of the two of them going together. I knew what she wanted me to say, so I told her I didn't care. This made her very happy and she told Kid everything would be okay. She said the rest of her kids would go along with it and that I was the only one she had been worried about. The rest of that trip is not even in my memory bank. I have no idea if we went up North or if we turned around and went back home. My mind shut down!

The only other incident I remember about Kid was at the house with the front porch. Buzzie, Kid, Rudy and myself had all been someplace together. It was dark when we got home and we pulled the car into the alley behind the house. Buzzie told me to go in and put on a pot of coffee. Rudy came in with me and soon the coffee was done. I went running out to tell her, feeling pretty good and thinking how we were bonding. Why she was even being nice to Rudy these days. "Hey the coffee is going to get cold", totally unprepared for her to scream at me like that. "Get back in that house and don't ever pull a stunt like this again". Confusion runs rampant! I sure could not figure Buzzie out, if I thought she would yell at me, she wouldn't and when I figured she was happy with me, she yelled at me. Soon after that night came the telegram and then--- Noreen.

Noreen was a friend of Buzzies I guess although she claimed Howard had run around with her. Noreen's husband was in the Navy and her little girl was about seven. The two of them needed a live in housekeeper and babysitter, since her husband would not be there. The money days were gone along with the Cartage business. We needed money, so Buzzie sent me to live with Noreen.

The live in nanny business was nothing new to me. The summer just before I had turned ten Howard and Buzzie had hired me out to a big farmer. His wife had just had a new baby and couldn't take it out to the fields yet. I cared for the baby and helped the Mother with meals, laundry and general cleaning. The farmers were a little hesitant about "my tender age" as they put it but Howard convinced them to give me a try, It worked fine and I stayed through the summer and potato-picking season.

The night the farmer drove me home to our farm was late in the month of October. My birthday was just a few days a way. "Your birthday present is out in the barn", said Howard and he handed me a flashlight to go look for it. As soon as I entered the barn I heard these new sounds emitting from a corner. Following those little baa-baa sounds I found this tiny baby goat. He was so cute, with brown spots here and there on his white body. He liked me, I liked him, Howard and Buzzie were pleased. It was a good birthday present. I named him Billy. Billy was all mine and I watered him, walked with him and fed him flowers. There was always a good reason to hurry home that winter. Like all things do though, Billy grew up. One day in early Spring when I came home from school Billy was gone, I just knew he was in packages in that big locker plant in town, I knew it, I felt it, but I don't remember ever asking, Nothing is forever, Even presents are only temporary gifts!

Back to Noreen. She was to pay me a small amount of money and I was to be her cook, housekeeper and baby-sitter. Her apartment was small and upstairs and I slept on a couch that pulled down and made a bed in the living room. There was a window in that room with a little metal balcony outside of it. I spent many wistful hours on that balcony when the girl wasn't awake, if she was awake she demanded every minute of my time, unless Noreen was home. Everyone else referred to the girl as a Navy brat or spoiled brat, not Noreen of course,

The girl would complain about every thing I did or said to her Mom. She didn't like the way I ate soup. So Noreen told me to look at the brat and follow her example. The soup spoon was to be pushed backwards in the bowl and then brought to your mouth. My singing bothered her, cutting my nails, even certain clothes I wore irritated that girl. Noreen sent me out to the patio a lot when she was home just so the girl wouldn't have to see me so much, It was fine with me. I could watch the people below and cars drive by. I would try to guess the year and the make of the cars. That was something Rudy and I used to do a lot in the house with the big front porch. I actually could tell most of the makes and model.

Down a few blocks from my balcony was a High School and Noreen told me in the fall I would attend it for my tenth year of schooling. I really looked forward to that. First of all that meant I wouldn't be with the brat so much and also I really liked school. Ninth grade had taught me things I never knew existed and I soaked it all in.

One teacher in ninth grade had been so kind to me. Her name was Miss Kemp and she always wore dresses with matching belts tied around her waist, only the belts didn't stay on her waist, they always climbed high up her back. Each morning I would check out Miss Kemps belt to see if it fit her, but it never did. I used to think Buzzie could have made her dresses that fit her much better. Miss Kemp was my homeroom teacher and also in charge of my Math class. She spent a big part of the home room time teaching us a poem that year. She said it was her biggest desire for every student to learn it. The poem goes like this.

I HAVE TO LIVE WITH MYSELF AND SO,
I WANT TO BE FIT FOR MYSELF TO KNOW.
I DON'T WANT TO KEEP ON A CLOSET SHELF,
A LOT OF SECRETS ABOUT MYSELF.
AND FOOL MYSELF AS I COME AND GO

INTO THINKING THAT NO ONE ELSE WILL KNOW.
I WANT TO BE ABLE AS DAYS GO BY,
ALWAYS TO LOOK MYSELF STRAIGHT IN THE EYE.

There was more, but today I can't remember it. That poem got to me then and became an inner strength to me hundreds of times. Thank you Miss Kemp. That wonderful teacher taught me the difference between stupidity and ignorance. She told me I excelled in intelligence and something called an IQ test proved it. She said I was in the genius range. She also tried to explain and even said she was sorry for having to use the "curve grading system" for our final marks that year. She said otherwise most of her students would have failed the class. But if she would have used the curve correctly for my English and Math marks they would have been over one hundred per cent, so she made them ninety-eight and ninety-nine. She was so proud of me and thanked me for not making her feel like a failure at teaching. I thought at that moment I was the luckiest girl in the world and decided I would be a teacher some day. The two people in this world who had been the nicest to me were teachers, not counting Grandma Ida.

The first teacher, Mrs. Blank, taught in the little two room school up by the farm. She had been the one to nurse me when my nose got mashed. She had poured cold water on my tongue when I stuck in on a frozen flag -pole and she trusted me to be in charge of her room when she had to leave it. I remember a note Mrs. Blank had sent home when I was off school for a long rime with something Buzzie referred to as a Mastoid.

The sickness itself is kind of a blur. At first I just had an earache on the left side. Buzzie would blow cigarette smoke in it at night and plug it with cotton, so the smoke would stay in I guess. Soon I was just sleeping most of the time and that was good because whenever I woke up it hurt too much. Grandma Ida came over to see me and that short little woman stood there yelling at her tall handsome son to get me into town to a doctor and get that thing lanced before it killed me. Howard usually listened to Ida. One other time she had yelled at him to take me to a doctor.

Half way down the cellar stairs in Ida and TJS house was a light bulb. You could screw the bulb and it would turn on. One time when I was sent on an errand to the cellar to get carrots if I remember correctly. TJ had carrots stuck in boxes of sawdust in his cellar and although they were a little soft they were edible even in the winter. He kept apples and potatoes down there also and lots of pickles and canned vegetables on shelves. This time I was going for carrots. When

I went to screw the light bulb either it was missing or broken because I didn't grab anything to turn. I fell down the cellar stairs in the dark with a lot of pain in my right thumb.

Buzzie would relate the story to people that it knocked me out and she soaked my hand in mud to draw out the electricity. I thought at the time Ida was yelling at Howard to take me for stitches. It is all confused in my mind, and it really doesn't matter. Just one more thing that I will never know the truth about. All I know today is I have a very ugly thumb with scars running down the inside and rough hard skin on the side by my fingers. The thumb is there and it works. Ida had thought it would be gone and I would look like Howard. You see his right thumb had been cut off when he worked in the Shoe Factory.

The relatives used to talk about Howards thumb too when us kids were doing our Sin and Evil bible study in Ida and TJS living room. They said things like "Howard probably cut his thumb off on purpose so that the Shoe Factory would give him money to buy the farm". I remember once TJ went in the kitchen and told the other relatives that they were like serpents with forked tongues. He said they talked one way to people's faces and another at their backs. He said if Howard came in right then everyone of them would be real nice to him to him and say only good things to his face. Some things are so hard to sort out. TJ did not talk a lot but what he did say always made so much sense to me. In his later years Howard reminded me a lot of TJ, especially in his talking. Perhaps because he talked so little that when he did it seemed monumental.

Anyway when Ida got real mad at Howard he usually listened and with this Mastoid business of mine he did listen and took me to the doctor. The doctor was not real happy and was saying quiet Swear words to Howard and Buzzie but he did cut the lump and soon after I started getting better.

Then came the note from my nice teacher Mrs. Blank. I cried heartbroken, sobbing tears when I read it, for it was saying she missed me and hoped I would get well fast but it also said I shouldn't even think about passing school this year. In my little ignorant mind that meant there was no chance of me passing. My little heart felt like it was breaking. Buzzie finally got me to understand that what Mrs. Blank really meant was there was no danger of me passing and not to even worry about it. I got well and went back to school and my nice Mrs. Blank hugged me. And passed me!

While living with Noreen I had lots of rules, a certain time to get up, a certain time to prepare meals and eat and a certain time for unrolling the couch bed and turning off the lights. I was allowed one night a week to go out with Rudy although sometimes he would walk by the patio and talk up to me. Once that summer Noreen planned a big vacation for herself and she would take me along. She talked about it for weeks. The brat was going to visit the Navy husbands parents for two weeks while her and I drove to California. She said the place where she worked would be shut down and several of her co-workers were going to meet her out there. She was very excited about it and bought us matching skirts. I really liked that skirt and wore it for many years!

The trip was long and we had to stop on the way to sleep, sometimes in little bedrooms on the side of the road and sometimes in her Studebaker car. Once we finally got to California and Noreen found her co-workers she became a different person. She laughed all the time, talked real nice to me and hugged and kissed everyone.

I remember the fire at the ocean on that trip. Everyone was singing, drinking beer and laughing a lot. On of her co-workers really seemed to like me, all of her co-workers were guys about Rudys age. In the dark there by the ocean Noreen went walking with some of her friends while this one guy sat by me. He kept trying to kiss me and put his hand on my breast. It was making me very nervous and I was always standing up and walking around telling him I was worried about Noreen. She did come back! When I told her about it on our way back to our little bedroom, by then I knew the correct name was a Motel, Noreen told me I was being silly and that the guy was just drinking.

It was strange, Buzzie had said the came thing to me years earlier when a similar thing had happened. That time I had been baby sitting some cousins when this uncle came home before any one else and climbed in bed with me and some of the cousins. He was feeling my chest (I didn't even have lumps there yet) and although I pretended to be asleep I was actually lying there praying the rest of the adults would hurry home. They did and so I knew if you prayed hard enough God listened. When I told Buzzie about that uncle she said the same thing Noreen was saying now, that he was just drinking. Okay, a mental note to myself "when guys drink alcohol they kiss girls and feel their breasts".

I begged Noreen to let me stay at the Motel the next day. She wouldn't hear of it she said and I should quit being such a baby. She said she would tell the guy how old I was and that would take care of the whole situation. She said the plan was to go to TiJuana the next day and that was the high point of the trip. No more discussion. I was just going. Oh, how I did not want to have to see that guy ever again. I prayed and prayed for Noreen to let me stay at the Motel instead. I must not have prayed hard enough because the next day we spent with her friends again. Maybe the guy wasn't drinking because he didn't touch me.

On the drive home from California Noreen would have me write postcards. She would tell me what to write while she drove. She still had rules for me though and I was only allowed to write two postcards to Rudy. She had me write three to him from herself. Later on Noreen told me that her and Rudy went out some times "just to pal around" is how she put it. When I asked Rudy about it he explained that since I could go out only once a week, it was good for him to go with Noreen so he could hear about me. It made sense to me at the time. How simple minded was I? In her dictated post cards that I wrote she told Rudy that I was a mute. Her explanation to me at the time was it meant I didn't talk much, but her laugh sounded strange when she said it.

Noreen picked up two Navy men who were hitchhiking on the trip home. She said she always felt sorry for Sailors because her husband was one. The Sailors rode with us all day and part of the night. After a gas stop the tall one sat up front with her and the little young one sat in the back with me. We had such good long talks and he actually seemed sad to leave me. When we got back to Noreen's Milwaukee home, there was a long letter from that Sailor. Noreen was not happy about it. She dictated one letter for me to write him and she wrote him one telling him I was only fourteen and lots of other things. Ray Thurmond never wrote me again, but I often thought of him.

School started and true to her word Noreen took me over to the new High School. She explained to the office why I would be going there and why I would not be coming to a Home Room in the morning because I needed to take her daughter to her school first. I didn't get to go to that school very long. All of a sudden there was a big panic. Noreen's husband was coming home from the navy and I would have to leave her place immediately.

I had two very close girlfriends from the first day I had started regular High School. One of the girls Mothers now invited me to come and live with them. Donna and I had shared the secrets of our souls and we were as close as we could be. It was a dream come true that her family would take me in. Buzzie had stayed with them for a while too. Donna and I did everything together. It was regular family life and we were like twins.

Donna had the funniest boyfriend, Steve. His name was really Stephen but everyone called him Steve because it sounded so much more American. Steve had just been in this country a few months. Him and his family had come from Germany and the way he talked was hilarious. He would get the words all mixed up and some would be in German and some in English. We could spend hours listening to Steve talk. After a while we decided he mixed up some words just because he knew it would make us laugh.

The family life at Donna's didn't last more than a couple of weeks. The word came by telephone that Buzzie and Howard were back together and would be coming for all their kids that weekend.

Ray/Punky had been living in Milwaukee on his own this whole time and the younger ones had been living with Howards brother. We were all gathered up and piled in an old car again for a new beginning.

THE SUN IS SHINING
OH HAPPY DAY
NO MORE TROUBLES
AND NO MORE SKIES OF GREY.

That hunk of song kept running through my head.

This new beginning was to take place in a new State. Illinois wasn't that far though. I could remember riding there for Oleo. That was something City people ate on their bread. When we lived on the farm we had put butter or lard on our bread but once we got citified we went to Illinois and bought this stuff called Oleo Margarine. It was white and was in a plastic bag. In the middle was a marble sized orange ball. You had to take the white bag and keep rolling it between your hands until the orange ball broke and the color ran out of it. If you rolled it long enough the whole bag full of stuff would turn yellow. Eventually it looked like butter and tasted more like the salted lard we used to eat. That's what I knew about Illinois as we headed off on our new beginning. No doubt singing at the top of our voices.

That first house in Illinois was very big, it had two floors and a big porch that went around two sides of it. We were going to be the only ones living in there. Howard and Buzzie already had paint cans sitting around and some of the upstairs rooms had been scrubbed and cleaned. Us kids were going to sleep upstairs. It was all so exciting. Howard and Buzzie had it all planned out. They were already working at jobs. Howard was delivering appliances and furniture for a big store and he had gotten Punky a job with him. Buzzie was working at a restaurant serving food. I was to stay home. Young Howie was too young for school yet and someone had to be home with him. They thought it was a perfect plan since I could cook, clean and care for the younger kids. I could continue painting on the new house too and everyone would be doing their part and things would be wonderful. Sure they knew I would miss school but everyone had to sacrifice for the good of the family. Oh yes, and now I was to tell everyone I was eighteen years old!

The siblings were told over and over again to say to any and everyone that I was eighteen or we would all be separated. Illinois had some strange law Howard said that wanted kids to be graduated, married or in school. He could not understand it. Why in Wisconsin he had quit school at eleven years old and it sure never hurt him or anyone else we knew. Actually, we didn't know many people who did spend their time in school. So I became eighteen and we became a family again.

Rudy used to drive to Illinois with a whole carload of our friends. We would have such fun! We soon learned where the swimming spots were and would spend whole Saturdays or Sundays there. Sometimes we would pile as many kids as could fit into Rudys car and go to a Drive-In Movie. The deal was, a whole carload could go for a dollar and we got our money's worth! Kids would even be hiding in the trunk of the car. Those were fun times but so much of the time I was really alone. I missed school and all my friends.

Before too long Rudy and Buzzie were talking about him coming to Illinois and moving in with us. Howard didn't like the idea but he finally gave in. Buzzie told him she was afraid I would leave them and go back to Milwaukee if I didn't have friends down there and I had no chance to meet any since I was just stuck at in the house all the time. She told him it would help with the money situation too, since Rudy would work and pay room and board. Buzzie always had someone paying room and board in Milwaukee.

There was a big pregnant girl who put peroxide on her hair to turn it almost white. The man named Arlo who would buy us kids food and candy and many relatives, especially uncles who had come to the city to look for jobs. Howard had never complained before that I knew of but he sure didn't like the idea of Rudy moving in with us. He finally gave in and Rudy joined our family. It took him a long time to find a job and Howard was always cussing about it, saying things like we sure didn't need another mouth to feed. Eventually Rudy did find work at a factory that made motors for boats.

The funny thing about Rudy was now he went back to Milwaukee most weekends. When he had lived there he spent most weekends by us, now that he lived in Illinois with us he went back to Milwaukee all the time. Seemed strange to me!

Sometimes I would get to go with Rudy and stay with Donna for the weekend. I always had so much fun with her and Steve. Steffen Feffer is what we called him sometimes. Him and Donna were talking marriage now and we would laugh about her becoming Mrs. Steffen Feffer.

My sister Mocky was three years younger than me and she couldn't remember much about the farm. I had to teach her how to clean and sew and to tell the truth. Apparently she didn't remember Grandma Ida either because one day she came home from the store with a bottle of cherries that she had not paid for. I did my best to impersonate the shameful scolding and sad look that Ida had given me so many years ago when I had taken that cookie from her pantry. I told Mocky I had expected more from her and never believed she would steal anything. Finally she started crying, it was then I marched her back to the store with the jar of cherries. I made her say she was sorry and that she would never take anything again. Mocky didn't like me for a while! Today she says I am her best friend and often talks of that time with the cherries. You see she wasn't even hungry. There was always food in that house in Waukegan Illinois. We lived there for a long time!

The next house was out of town a ways, closer to the city of Zion where Howard and Ray (I did finally get used to calling my brother by his given name) worked.

We were going to buy the new house. The people who had owned it could not make the payments any longer and were going to sell it to us for a small down payment and move back to where ever they had come from. That whole family sat in our driveway one day eating bologna sandwiches and waiting for Howard to come home with money to give them. Buzzie was real angry at me for not inviting them in but I swear I didn't know who they were. I had never seen them before and they did not tell me who they were. The man had just knocked on the door and asked if Howard was there. I told him that he should be home any minute and so they sat and waited. The man could tell that I was in big trouble and so he told my folks that I had indeed invited them in but they declined my invitation. Yes, it was a lie but he was trying to keep me out of trouble. Is that what they call a White lie?

School was over for the year now so Mocky could watch Squeak and young Howard. I was hired out to a family back in the city of Waukegan. This mans name was Frenchy and he was an entertainer (a piano player) and his wife was a waitress with Buzzie. I did the usual stuff, cleaning, cooking and taking care of the two little kids. I slept on a cot in the kid's room.

Rudy was back in Milwaukee because the boat motor factory (it had a name now, Johnson Motors) had laid him off and Howard would not let him live with us if he didn't pay room and board. Howard still didn't like Rudy and never had a nice thing to say about him. Sometimes when Frenchy or his wife were off work Rudy would drive down and take me to visit my family. Once in a while Howard and Ray would have a delivery close by and they would stop by Frenchy's house for a cup of coffee, but mostly I was just by myself that summer. When the school year started I went back to the family house in Zion.

Young Howie was old enough to start school now and money was a problem. There was a factory in the city of Zion that made Televisions. It had been decided I would go to work there. First though I would have to get something called a Social Security Card.

Howard drove Buzzie and me to this big building where the "blankity blank government officials" were as he put it. I was very nervous as Buzzie told those government officials the story. She said a doctor had come to her house the night I was born but he died soon after and had never recorded a birth certificate for me. She told the person behind the desk that I was eighteen now and she needed a Social Security Card for me. They gave me one!

With my brand new card in hand we went to the Television factory and Buzzie and I were both given jobs. It was strange but exciting too. I liked the work and all the people. Buzzie only stayed a few weeks at the Television factory. She said that kind of work made her sick and she would go back to waitressing. I was to work there for two years that time. At first I had a fear of someone finding out my true age and kicking me out of the factory. Many times when a boss would come up behind me I would believe he was going to take me by the shoulders and guide me right out the front door. The longer I was working the less often I was fearful and soon it was a comfort to be at the factory. It was so nice to be out meeting people and making friends.

Howard had decided I could keep part of the check the television factory gave me every week. It seems like it was five dollars a week but I'm not sure. Howard and Buzzie needed money very badly. They were always talking about money or lack of it these days. I never learned why but it probably had something to do with buying the house we were living in. Always before we had just cleaned and painted apartments to pay for living there and now we had to pay someone money.

Things at home were getting very sour again. Some fights were about money but many more were about some guy with a long Italian name. Then the fights would be about all the things from the past. I would lie there at night hearing them screaming at each other about everything from the farm, Madeline, Kid

Smith and this new Italian name. They would take turns spending nights away from home and I was so happy I had the factory to go to every day. I knew the end was coming soon. I was totally unprepared for how it occurred. No one could be prepared for that!

The folks had been fighting real badly one night when all of a sudden things got quiet. Buzzie sat in the living room of our house in Zion and Howard went into the kitchen. I could hear him sobbing at the kitchen table and then he called my name. That sight is etched in my mind forever as the most traumatic thing in my life.

There was blood all over the floor and running off both of Howards wrists. I started screaming and shaking but I couldn't move. Buzzie finally came into the kitchen. She was yelling at me to call for an ambulance but I couldn't move. Somehow the ambulance came and I still couldn't move. Howard was saying not to worry as they took him away and I still hadn't moved. Buzzie was worried about me and asked the ambulance guys what to do. They must have told her to get me warm because she laid me down and put lots of blankets on me. I could not stop shaking!

Somehow she got me moving again and she started talking about what we would have to do. We would move back to Waukegan where she could walk to her waitress job. There was a bus that ran between the two cities so I could continue to work at the factory. The plans were made and carried out swiftly. We wouldn't be seeing Howard for a very long time, Buzzie said, so we had to figure out how to survive with out him.

You know, I can't remember Rudy at the house in Zion. I don't know if he was laid off again and staying back at his parents house in Milwaukee or if because so much was going on in my life, what

Howard hitchhiked down to see his first grandchildren get baptised.

with the job and Howards suicide attempt that I just didn't notice him. When we moved back to Waukegan Rudy was back in my memory bank. He was no longer the only person I knew outside of the family now.

There were other people I saw every day at the factory and we had fun. We would all sit together at break time with our coffee bought from machines. We would smoke our cigarettes, drink coffee and share stories. Sometimes we would all bring food and cake from home and sing Happy Birthday to whoever had a birthday. I had money now because instead of giving Buzzie all my check and her giving me back a few dollars I got to keep most of my money. The new arrangement was to pay her fifteen dollars a week. It was just like a grown up person paying Room and Board. What fun that was! Mocky and I went shopping all the time.

My sister was growing up and she needed things. I bought her Bras and silk underpants. She had started her period and I bought her sanitary pads at the store. I didn't want her to ever have to wash those slimy bloody rags. We were pals, Mocky and me. She confessed to me that Rudy had taken her out riding some times and stopped on an old logging trail-- "-to teach her how to kiss" is how she put it. I don't think I liked that much but Rudy claimed he was just being nice to her because she was worried about being able to attract boys. Rudy was 20 years old and Mocky was 13. In today's society he would spend many years in jail for what he did with her and actually with me also since I was still only 16 years old. How strange it seems to me today that I accepted everything he said then. He always convinced me he was much smarter because he was so much older and after all he was a High School graduate. I can't even count how many times He repeated that phrase to me.

Mocky really liked Rudy's younger brother but he looked at her like a little girl and strictly called her Tug Boat. So Rudy was trying to help her be more grown up or so he claimed. (A note to the reader)----- I offer no judgment here or more information than what I have already shared with you. If the reader wishes to try to understand it better. I leave it to their discernment as I have so many incidents in these pages. To say I understood all the things that were going on in my life would be a complete and utter falsehood. Even looking back today, I can't understand!

Buzzie seemed happy and we had company quite often. I don't remember ever going to visit Howard in the hospital after he slashed his wrists. She said he had been sent to a Veterans (vetrins is how Buzzie used to say it) Hospital in Downey Illinois. Sometimes she referred to the hospital as a place for the criminally insane, other times she would say it was a nice hospital for Veterans and that the government should give good care to Howard after him serving in the Marine Corps.

That's right, I remember when he was in the Marines. Now that part of our lives came back to me. We were very young when Howard was in "The Service". There were only three of us kids in those days. The country was at war and all the young men were being drafted. Howard was no exception. He knew he would soon have to go. Instead of letting the Army draft them; Howard, his brother and a friend signed up for the Marines. The only one who stayed in the Marines his full term was the friend. Howard's brother was "honorably discharged" in a few months. That was important for all the young men to have their return home papers say "honorably discharged".

Howard was gone for over a year before he was "honorably discharged. Why, I don't know. Oh I heard lots of different stories but every area of our lives had different stories, depending on who was doing the talking and if Buzzie was the only one talking it still would be different from time to time. She said most times that he had his back injured.

What I think I remember was living in the town of Antigo in a house on Weed Street. How appropriate, almost poetic that we, the weeds should live on a street named Weed. Those days, those months, on Weed Street were strange even for people like us. There were so few men around so most of the work was done by women. If cars were driven at all, it was a woman behind the wheel, mostly the cars just sat still though. Buzzie would tell us it was because the gas was rationed. It seemed like everything was rationed on Weed Street.

The women would complain that their bare legs got so cold because they could not have stockings. They were rationed. We could not have sugar on our cereal because it was rationed. The women could not drink coffee because it was rationed. Instead of coffee they would get jars of some dark brown powder and put teaspoons of it in cups of hot water. A poor substitute they would say, but they drank it.

Once in a while Buzzie would get a little book with tear out pages in it. We could take the pages with us to the store and buy things. Those were days for celebration because we could have sugar and coffee again. Soon the book would be empty though and we would have to wait for the next ration. I never learned where those little books came from.

Buzzie had a good friend who lived right across the street from us and a sister who lived close by. Us kids spent a lot of time with both of those people because

Buzzie had to work, I guess. Our Aunt Sadie was a stern woman but always good to us kids. She had a daughter my age and we were pals. That is the only time in my memory that we spent much time with Buzzies family, except for the real early years with her parents. Grandma Webster died while we lived on Weed Street. Howard got to visit us because of the funeral. He got to visit us several other times too.

He came home one time with a whole mouthful of store bought teeth and another time he had what us kids thought were balloons. We sure got in big trouble for taking those balloons outside and blowing them up. Howard and Buzzie were both yelling and cursing at us. Years later Buzzie would tell us storie's about those balloons, if she were mad at Howard at the time. She claimed he had so many girlfriends that he got diseased. She said he had something else too. She called it Pyorrhea of the mouth and that is why the Marine Coup pulled all his teeth and gave him store bought ones. He supposedly had lain in the hospital twice too, for long periods of time. One time because his Appendix had burst and poison was inside his body. Another time it was an injury to his back.

Each time Howard came to visit us it seemed like him and Buzzie spent the whole visit fighting and

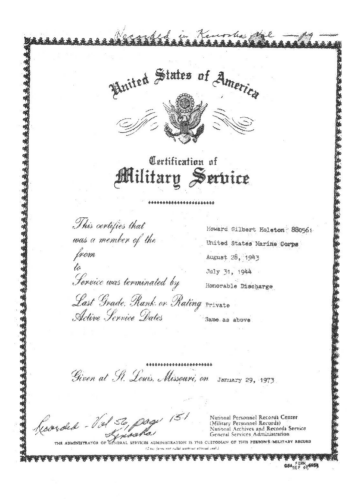

cursing each other out. He said all bad things about her family, she said all bad things about his family and they both ran around. Us kids ran too, barefoot and wild through the streets and alleys of Antigo.

Sometime in that era my sister Squeak was born. I heard Buzzie say many times that Squeak was a twin but the other twin was born dead. I heard, from some of the fights, that Squeak's Father was not Howard. Squeak heard it too and it would haunt her all of her life. Many times Squeak would get real sad and wonder who her Dad was. Sometimes Buzzie would tell her that Howard really was her Father and that she only told him that he wasn't because she wanted to hurt him. Poor sister Squeak didn't know what story to believe.

I only know she is my sister and I love her so very much. I wish she would never have had to hear those stories. She never got over them and she never got to know Howard. She was afraid of him. Whenever he was around, Squeek was uncomfortable. If you ask my baby sister what her biggest hurt, her most traumatic experience in life was, she would always answer, without hesitation. It was being told that Howard was not her father. Poor Squeek!

We continued to live on Weed Street even after the Marine Corps honorably discharged my father. It seems like a lot of the woman worked in a shoe factory making boots for the service men and soon after his discharge Howard went to work there too. Those are the memories of the days of the Marine Corps in my mind. And now Howard was in a Veterans Hospital and the rest of us were living in Waukegan.

My job was becoming the best part of my life. I really was enjoying my new friends. Buzzie was always telling me to get rid of Rudy and to tell the truth I was very tired of him and his bossy ways. He didn't like any of my friends from the factory and for sure did not want me to talk about them. All Rudy wanted to do was drink beer and talk about himself.

Sometimes we would leave the factory on our half-hour lunch break and go to a restaurant. One young man liked me, I could tell because he didn't just talk about himself like Rudy did, he actually wanted me to talk to him about my feelings. He reminded me of Ray Thurmond, that nice Sailor that had talked to me on the trip to California. He asked me what I wanted to do with my life. It's funny I didn't think anyone had ever asked that before. I told him about my old dream of becoming a teacher but I would never be able to do that because I didn't have any education to speak of. He asked what sort of man I wanted to marry. When I said I hadn't thought about it, he said I should think about it and if and when I did, would I think about him? This guy from Mississippi was so wonderful, he hadn't even tried to kiss me. Of course I went straight home and told Buzzie. "See", she said "there are lots of nice guys out there but you will never know them with that Albatross around your neck", she meant Rudy of course.

When the factory shut down for vacation I was sad to think I would not see any of my friends for two weeks. The very first day of vacation I told Rudy that I was thinking of other guys therefore I must not be in love with him. I wanted to break up with him and I wanted him to quit living with us. He refused to go and instead argued with me for days. He told me again how much smarter he was than I was, after all he had a high school education and he was so much older and wiser than I was. He said I was too young to know what I wanted. The people at the factory were turning me against him and without him I would be just like Buzzie with one boyfriend after another. He said the people at the factory would have nothing to do with me if they knew how old I really was. On and on went Rudy. He argued and argued but I stood firm on my decision.

Rudy went back to his parents in Milwaukee. Things were happy now! Mocky and I shopped. Buzzie and I talked and I eagerly looked forward to my return to the factory. Then came the telegram! Rudy's brother was coming down to our house at such and such a time. He needed to talk to me the telegram said. We didn't like the sound of it and Buzzie was there with me when the brother arrived. She wanted to keep me strong in my decision.

The picture he painted in our minds was pretty sadistic. He claimed that Rudy was standing in front of moving cars and they had wrestled knives away from him. Rudy was trying to commit suicide the brother said and at the moment was laying in a coma back in his parents home. Memories of Howard sitting in the kitchen with the blood everywhere a few months earlier flooded my head. Buzzie tried to harden my heart or make me stronger. The brother was begging me to go see him, Buzzie was saying if I went I world never be free of him. She said that his whole family would gang up on me and convince me to go back with Rudy. Good grief, the jumble of thoughts in my head--- Howard, Buzzie, Rudy, the factory, the family, the suicide threats. The brother was promising Buzzie and me he would drive me right back home if I would just go talk to Rudy. I went!!!

Rudy's parents house had all the shades pulled down when we arrived. The rest of the family sat in the little living room looking at the open door of the parent's bedroom. In the bedroom lay Rudy in his supposed Comatose State. As soon as he heard me ask where he was, a miracle happened. (sure). He was fully awake and well. He couldn't live without me, did I want that on my conscience and on, and on, and on. He got up out of bed and we took the train back to Waukegan.

The next day Rudy and I left Buzzies house for Mississippi to get married. That was a state that

Rudy said would let sixteen year old's get married without parental consent. That black car we drove to Mississippi was nicknamed Tugboat (I never knew if the car was named after Mocky or if Mocky was called Tugboat after the car) all I knew was the car only had two gears, second and third. The trip and the ceremony didn't seem real to me. I kept thinking my handsome Howard would never allow this to happen to me. Why at any moment he would pop up and save me. I looked for him all day long. Howard never came!

We got married early on a Monday morning and sat in a hotel lobby most of the day waiting for Buzzie to telegraph us money. Rudy had a check waiting for him at the Outboard Motor factory and had made arrangements for her to pick it up. She must have had trouble getting the check because the money didn't arrive until late afternoon. There was never before or never since, a day so long. My mind was completely saturated with sadness. I was supposed to have gone back to my job, my beloved job, this morning. There was supposed to have been a new beginning to my life. I was supposed to be free of my Albatross. It was all gone! Howard hadn't saved me.

The money finally arrived, we paid the hotel guy for the meal he had given us on credit and headed back for Wisconsin. Rudy took a picture of me standing by the road sign as we left the city. The rest of the trip is just a blur in my memory. I know we spent Monday night in a Motel in a different state and I know we got back to Buzzies house late on Tuesday. She said we could sleep on her bed and the next day Rudy would have to rent us an apartment. It was like all these events were happening to someone else. It just couldn't be real. Wednesday morning I got up early to get ready for work. Buzzie made me promise to stop at the drugstore on the way home from work. "Buy some Norform suppositories" she said "and use them". She didn't want me to be having any babies at least. I did it!

My factory friends were happy to see me and said they had been worried about me. That wonderful young man from Mississippi looked sad and later on stopped by my work area. All he said was "did you have to get married"? At that moment I assumed he meant was I pregnant so I answered his question with a no. He seemed taken aback by my answer but said nothing else. We didn't talk again for months.

The apartment Rudy had rented for us was in Zion. He had it all figured out he said. It was only about a mile to my factory so I could walk to work. He had the car so when his factory called him back to work he would drive. The apartment had three rooms and all the furniture we needed. I had bought a television set from my work some time ago and they took payments for it out of my paycheck. So we really were all moved in.

Rudy was looking for a different job sometimes because he had been laid off for a long time and he worried he would run out of unemployment. Then he went to see the doctor and had a hernia operation. The factory paid him checks for the summer now!

I didn't get to see my family much these days because the bus only ran between the two cities at certain hours and those were the hours I worked. Rudy saw them quite often though. At least the kids, it was hot that summer so they went swimming a lot. Sometimes him and Mocky and/or Punky would go to Milwaukee to see his family or friends. I didn't care. I wasn't feeling so good these days.

Maybe it was because the little apartment was so hot or perhaps I was just sad. One day I told Buzzie about my breasts being sore and that I hadn't had my period since getting married. She told me it was natural in newly married women but gave me a doctor's name and how to get to see him. Rudy was spending a lot of time in Milwaukee recuperating from his hernia operation. It was too warm for him to be coped up in that little apartment he said, so I was alone a lot.

I took the bus to the doctor. That day is almost as unreal to me as the day months before, in Mississippi. What was that strange doctor saying "You are going to have a baby young lady. Very politely I told him he must be wrong because my mother had told me how to prevent that from happening. I had never forgotten to use my drug store medicine, not one time did I miss. No, he went on "I am not wrong, you are about ten weeks pregnant young lady". Now from me came the quiet little "are you sure"? He was sure and now he talked soothingly to me. I had something else too, something about "toxemia" but not to worry, it was not real unusual in such young girls and with the right food and medication I would be fine. He explained how we would guess the actual day the baby would be born. He said baby's took about seven days less than nine months to be born so we would take my wedding night, add nine months, subtract the seven days and that would be it.

Boy was my head spinning, on April fourth I would become a Mother, according to this strange Doctor. I got on the bus but instead of taking it back to the apartment in Zion I went to Buzzies house. I knew in my heart Rudy would be mad about that, because he always wanted to know everything first, but I couldn't help it. On this day I wanted my Mother!

At first Buzzie was sad but we talked a lot and then we both started getting happy about it all. A baby was on it's way. Her little girl would soon be a Mother and she would be a Grandmother. I told her I wished Howard were there. She said he would be home soon. The hospital said he was well and would be released in a few days. It turned out to be a happy day after all.

Howard came home from the hospital and him and Buzzie decided to make a new beginning in Milwaukee. I could picture the happy scene with everyone riding off in the car, singing, but I was no longer a part of that group. Rudy and myself had to get ready for the baby. The factory had rules about pregnant women. They could only work for five months, take a maternity leave and return six weeks after the baby was born. I was so sure I would never work after I had the baby that I just quit. I didn't want to ever leave my children like I had been left.

Rudy said the apartment cost too much money for one person to pay for. Rudy always took care of the money. From the day we married I had to give him my check and he gave me back an allowance. That's just the way it was supposed to be and after all he was older, wiser and had a high school education, again I had to hear that. He rented a tiny place in Waukegan that was real cheap. It was just one room with a skinny place (kind of like a closet) that held a stove and a refrigerator. The landlord lived above us and talked a foreign language. That man frightened me because he was always yelling about something. One time I was in the basement using the washing machine, which was allowed, but he was yelling at me anyway. It took a while to understand enough half English words before I knew why he was so angry. It was Saturday or Sunday (I'm not sure which) and in his house no work could be done on this day. We were heathens and he wanted us to move. Actually we would have had to move soon anyway since my belly could hardly fit into the skinny place by the stove and refrigerator now.

The next apartment was upstairs from a dear old lady in her seventies. You could see the factory where Rudy worked from the front windows. It was big and it was empty.

I remember the day Buzzie and Rudy's Mother came down with all the stuff. There was a wooden rocking chair, a two burner hot plate and a mattress. They knew for sure it wasn't good or right for someone so pregnant to be sleeping on the bare floor. Things were looking better. A big cardboard box turned upside down with the hotplate on top became my stove and I loved the rocking chair. Many hours were spent in that rocking chair crocheting little things for my baby.

That old dear from downstairs taught me how to read pattern books and I made things constantly. She shared yarn with me and stories. She was a good friend. In fact she was my only friend. At first a few girlfriends from the factory came to see me but Rudy was not nice to them at all. They quit coming to see me and soon it was just Mable and me.

Mable and I had a lot of time on our hands. She had to walk with a cane and it was hard for her to climb stairs so I spent a lot of time in her apartment. Sometimes I would walk downtown and shop for her. She always wanted to pay me or do something for me. I didn't want her money, she was my friend, sometimes I would accept some yarn or crochet cotton. The walking was part of my daily routine anyway. The doctor still talked of Toxemia and walking was good for keeping it under control. He also told me what to eat and it seemed like I was existing on grapefruit at the time.

Sometimes on Friday night's we would go to Milwaukee and stay until Sunday. I loved those weekends. Rudy would drop me by my parents house and he would go by his family or friends. He knew Howard didn't like him and the feeling was mutual. Howard had told him in no uncertain terms that the marriage should never have taken place and it certainly would not have if he had been around to stop it. I just knew it, if only he would have been around, but then I would not be looking forward to becoming a Mommie.

On one trip to Milwaukee Buzzie had a baby shower for me. It seemed like everyone I knew was there. All my old school friends, Rudy's Mother and sisters and they all gave me things for the baby. It was so wonderful, I cried! Buzzie had bought yards and yards of flannel too and her and I cut and hemmed it for diapers. Towards the end of my pregnancy the doctor told me I could not travel any more. That was a very lonely time. I would fold each little baby thing over and over and cry. It seemed like I did that a lot these days. I would think about my old life and cry. I would look out the window and wonder when Rudy was coming home and cry. I was an emotional mess.

It seemed like Rudy didn't like me much. In fact from the moment we had married he changed his actions toward me. Now that I had this big belly it was obvious to everyone. Once I had even overheard Rudy's Father talking to him about the way he was treating me. Father was saying pregnant women were beautiful and had a special glow about them. Rudy said he just couldn't help it and said I was not the same person any more. He was just anxious to get this whole pregnancy thing over with and see if things would get back to normal. He said I just wasn't any fun anymore. Father scolded him but Rudy was firm. In his defense I'm sure he hadn't planned on having a family so soon either.

Rudy was right, I wasn't fun anymore and he liked having fun. He liked to be with the younger kids. They would "scoop the loop" which simply meant driving back and forth through the city looking at and talking to all the people. He liked going to carnivals and taking all the rides, I could no longer do that. He liked parties with lots of dancing and lots of beer, I could no longer do that. It was hard on him too I figured.

Rudy always took lots of pictures but now he took them of other girls. Mocky was his favorite person to take pictures of. He took dozens of pictures of her. Sometimes he had her put on my maternity clothes and took pictures of her.

When I could no longer go to Milwaukee with Rudy anymore I got pretty lonesome. One time Rudy brought Mocky back with him so she could spend some time with me. I'm not sure if she had quit school or if it was Easter vacation. She was fourteen years old. It was April and we were counting days.

A few days after Mocky came down Rudy was very late coming home. Mind you, he was late often because he liked to stop and have a few beers after working hard all day but this day he was very late. He was so sorry and ashamed he said because he had spent most of his check. There was a carnival in town and he had been trying to win both of us girls a big teddy bear. He had finally won just one bear. He gave it to Mocky! His logical explanation was he wanted me to forget about this night as soon as possible and if I had the teddy bear to look at it would make me remember it more. He was wrong!

I never argued with Rudy because I had promised myself that my life was not going to be full of arguments and loud voices for my children to hear. So outwardly I agreed with most anything he would say. Inside it hurt and my stomach would get knotted up in pain. One other time that week I awoke to see Rudy standing by the side of the mattress Mocky was sharing with me. He had the blanket lifted off her. I quietly got up and went out to the kitchen. There was nothing going on he said in response to my question. He said that men just have needs and he was only looking, not touching. He said I would never understand. He was right on that point, I would never understand. He was twenty-one years and she was fourteen, my sister and my closest friend.

There wasn't much time to think about that though because I wasn't feeling good. The cramps in my back and stomach were trying to consume me.

It was the eighth of April, already past the day the doctor had said the baby was due. I asked Mocky to go downstairs by Mable's and let Buzzie know just how I was feeling. Buzzie said the baby would be coming today or tomorrow and she was going to come by us. That made me so happy I wanted to cry. By late afternoon Buzzie and Howard came down. Mocky would go back with Howard to watch the younger kids and Buzzie would go to the hospital with us.

All night we waited, Rudy, Buzzie and me. There wasn't much talking, sometimes I would look over at Buzzie and watch her crocheting a little hat for the baby. It made me happy that I had taught her how to crochet. She had taught me so many things. When it was Rudy's turn to be in the room with me he would sleep on a chair sitting up. We didn't have anything to say to each other. He was sleeping in his chair when I said the baby was coming. He quickly called the nurse. The nurse lifted the blanket from me, took one look and called another nurse, they pushed me out, bed and all. That's all I remember!

April ninth the nurse brought my little girl to me to start the nursing procedure. Only a Mother could understand the overwhelming tidal wave of love. My life had meaning, I would never be alone, I would love her forever, she would love me forever. And Buzzie! I had never loved her more. To think she went through this process to give birth to me. It was almost too emotional!

It had been decided beforehand by Rudy to name her after Mocky and that is the name Rudy had them put on the birth certificate. But in my heart and mind she was and always will be my April Joy. She was perfect. She was beautiful and-----her eyes were crossed. I told the nurse, I told Buzzie. They both assured me it was only a temporary thing with new borns and her eyes would soon focus. April Joy completed me. I was a woman, I was a Mother, and now I knew why I had been put on this earth.

Rudy took Buzzie back to Milwaukee and was so proud. He bought cigars and drinks for everyone he knew. He sent me flowers.

Buzzie came back down to stay with me when I came home from the hospital. She read about a used washing machine in the newspaper. She talked loud to Rudy and told him to go and get it. She said I couldn't keep up with baby clothes, washing them in the bathtub like I had been ours and she wasn't even going to try. He left to go get the washing machine and I felt kind of bad, I told her that Rudy did not have money to buy things. Buzzie was still talking loud and said "he doesn't have to go drinking all the time. One or two days without his beer would pay for that five dollar washer". She was probably right but Rudy loved to drink beer. More than taking pictures, more than fourteen old girls, more than carnivals and more than April Joy, Rudy loved beer. He came back with a washing machine and I thanked him. It would be so nice! I couldn't see how washing those little bitty things in the tub would be hard but Rudy's blue jeans had always been hard to wring out. Life was good! Buzzie stayed a couple of days and then I was on my own.

I rocked her in the wooden rocker. She came outside with me while I hung up the clothes. I nursed her, loved her and watched her eyes. They stayed the same, crossed!

We would take trips to Milwaukee on the week-ends again, the three of us. The baby and I would stay by Buzzie and Howards. I don't know if Rudy slept there or not. I have no memories of him being there. Him and my parents were not on the same wave length at all. They thought he shouldn't drink so much and play so much and he thought they were wrong about almost everything. I loved them and missed my friends and family more than ever now.

I had thought the baby was all I would ever need but I was wrong. I would get so frightened sometimes about how to take care of her. One time I rushed her to the doctor because she was breathing funny. It was just some lint in her nose from her new clothes. I worried a lot and wished I had someone to get advice from once in awhile. My Mother, his Mother, or Donna. Donna had two children already. Rudy liked to be in Milwaukee all the time too and one day he said that if we had three hundred dollars, we would move back.

It was decided. The baby would be six weeks old and I would go back to work. Mocky would come and live with us for the summer and baby-sit little April. Every penny would be saved and in September we would move to Milwaukee. The biggest problem was where would I work since I hadn't taken advantage of the maternity leave at the television factory. When I had left six months earlier I had been so sure I would not come back that I said goodbye forever.

Now Rudy wanted me to car-hop at this Root Beer stand. He really liked the uniforms there. The orange and brown skirts were very short and they wore hats. I applied for the job and even came home with a uniform but I couldn't make myself do it. The next day I took the bus back to Zion and my old factory. Yes, of course they had a job for me. What a shame I hadn't taken the maternity leave because I would have been paid for the last six weeks. How happy they were to see me and how lucky they felt to have me return.

I don't know if I told them it would only be for three or four months.

The man from Mississippi didn't say much, only hello and that I was awfully skinny. "Are you well?" and I told him I was both well and happy. We never spoke again until the day I left the factory in September. He was sure right about me being thin. I had only gained eleven pounds carrying April and by now had lost about twenty-five. I would stay skinny for the next six years except when I had a big belly.

The summer passed quickly. I would nurse little April at six in the morning and take the bus to work at six thirty. Rudy did not want to drive me to work because he would have had to get up a half hour earlier. The way it was he could be to work in 10 minutes. In preparation for Mocky to care for April I had been giving her a bottle at ten in the morning and again at two in the afternoon. The other times I was home to nurse her.

It all worked well and soon it was time to move. I'm not sure why Rudy, Mocky and April had already gone back to Milwaukee but the last day at the factory I was to catch a train in Zion and ride it to Milwaukee. The man from Mississippi offered me a ride to the train. I declined his offer. He said he wished things had turned out differently. I told him I was only sixteen at the time that he spoke to me. He said "that wouldn't have mattered". I left the factory and walked to the train. It was going to be a new beginning. I would try very hard not to think of the factory or the man from Mississippi.

The house Rudy had rented was touching the sidewalk, it had four rooms downstairs, an attic and one more room upstairs. One side touched the alley and the side by the door was all concrete. There were clotheslines over the concrete. Not a blade of grass by that little house and the kitchen was a step lower than the other rooms. Little April tripped one time on that step. She had both hands in her pockets walking out of her bedroom at the time and fell right on her chin. She needed two stitches to sew it up.

There was a church across the street from this little house and a grocery store just a few blocks away. It was home for two and a half years for Rudy, April and me. Less than two years later little Michael was born. I loved being a Mom!

Rudy did construction work with his Father only his job was called Sheet Metal and his Fathers was called Iron Work. They put up buildings and worked out of town often. In the winter or rainy weather they couldn't work. There never seemed to be any money. I found a new factory job! So much for never leaving my children but Rudy just nagged me all the time because he said he could not help it if he was layed off so much and unemployment only went so far. I was supposed to do my part.

The new factory was named Briggs and Stratton and it was really big. In one part of that big factory we made motor parts (a machine shop they called it) and in another part we made locks and keys. The faster you could work at Briggs and Stratton the more money they paid you. They called peace work. I was young and fast so I made lots of money. For some reason the older ladies would get mad about that and soon one of them would have my job. The boss would come and tell me I had been "bumped" to a different job.

The last job at Briggs and Stratton was in the machine shop. I would have to wear rubber boots, gloves and a big rubber apron. I was grinding pistons on a big machine that had actual diamond tips on it. Sparks were always flying and water ran over the machines to keep them cool. I could make a lot of pistons and made good piece work money. This job no one bumped me off of. It seemed liked no one liked the noise, the hot sparks or the water. Also it was on the night shift and that was not real popular. The only thing I didn't like was the smell. It started to really make me sick. I was always throwing up. I would have to shut the big machine down and run for the bathroom several times a night.

Yes!---Michael was born on a cold February day. It was exactly the day the Doctor had predicted. The water bag sprung a leak early in the morning. It didn't gush out like some women said it does. It just dripped all day long. I wasn't in severe pain and did not want me to spend any more time in the hospital than I had too.

It seems like Rudy hadn't worked enough hours that year to have insurance coverage. The plan was to stay home as long as possible and come back home quickly too, so the hospital bill would be smaller. Plans are made to be broken I guess. The water was gone, the baby's head was very large and I developed infection, possibly because of the "dry birth" the Doctor said. The Doctor refused to sign a release form for me to leave the hospital the next day. But Rudy was yelling that we had no money so I just had to go. Rudy and I had to both sign a paper saying we wouldn't hold the Doctor responsible and that it was strictly against his or the hospitals wishes. They circumcised my boy and we went home.

It's strange looking back now. There was never a doubt in my mind that he would be a boy. Was I possibly so naive that it didn't occur to me that you didn't always get the sex you asked for. I don't know. I just knew that I would have a boy baby and his name would be Michael Dennis or Dennis Michael. Rudy said we could name him Michael but we had to use Lee for a middle name, after my sister Squeak who was thirteen at the time. People used to ask him why his first born was named after Mocky so now if he named one after Squeak maybe they would quit. Tuesday we left the hospital with baby and came home to little April. She was almost two and so sweet.

On Sunday I cooked a big meal and lemon pies for a lot of friends and family members. Rudy wanted to celebrate and show off his son. I didn't complain. It didn't work to ever complain to Rudy about anything. He knew he was always right and could spend hours telling you why he was right. Life was easier if I just dressed, acted and did every thing the way he wanted. People (friends and relatives from both families) would often ask me how I cold stand it. I would reply that it was easier for me to do what he wanted than listen to his drunken lectures besides he really wasn't around the house that much. His bars, his out of town job and his fun took up most of his time.

If.--- If he had been nicer to me. If-- he wouldn't have liked young girls so much. If--- he had been home more. If ---he wouldn't have gotten falling down drunk so often. If--- he had given me any money.

116

If--- he had ever changed a dirty diaper. If--- he would have worked more. If--- he would have been nicer to my baby's. If---he didn't constantly criticize me or tell me what a waste I would be without him. If--- I wouldn't have had to run scared for the lipstick and curlers before he came in the door. If--- he wouldn't have told me about all the pretty women out of town who thought he was wonderful and that I was so lucky to have him. If--- he wouldn't have been critical and jealous of all Mocky's boyfriends. If ---just a few of these if's were not if's would I, could I have been able to stay true to my promise. Only God knows!

All I knew then was it was getting harder and harder to find anything about him that I could admire. Maybe if I found more to do, more to occupy my mind. That was it, I would keep so busy there would be no time left to think. The babies and work were a lot but I still was missing something.

The first thing I started, was going to church. A couple of times I would walk clear across town to that church Rudy had taken me to when I was fourteen because he thought that was the best place to go. After all it was the Church where his family went. He wouldn't give me a ride and it took a long time to do all that walking so I stopped going there, instead I walked right across the street from our house and talked to a Pastor. We became friends, in a way. He taught me lessons and I helped with clean up and refreshments at the membership instruction lessons. Within a couple of months we were baptized into the Lutheran Church. My April, my Michael and me.

Next I studied for a drivers license and anyone who stopped to visit was begged to just let me drive a little, right in front of house even. I needed to practice for my road test. It was at this stage of my life that I needed a birth certificate. I had never had one!

The helpful people at the drivers licensing place told me to get three people to sign statements saying they personally knew I was born on that date. They had to swear to a Notary Public that they personally knew my parents were Howard and Buzzie. I can only remember the one Aunt who went with me to the government building. The other two people are lost in my brain some where. In the mail a few days later came my very own birth certificate. There it was in black and white, my parents names, my name and the correct year I was born but the date was November first. I will never know if Buzzie had told another story about me being born on Halloween or if someone made a mistake. It was a fun thing anyway. Someone stated it meant that I went from the witch's birthday to the All Saint's Birthday since all my life I had celebrated on Halloween and now it was November 1st which is all Saints day.

With my birth certificate in hand and Rudy's Mother at the wheel of her car we went for my road test and my drivers license. What a happy day and what a big milestone in my life. Rudy's Mother was almost as happy as I was.

I stayed busy. I sewed and crocheted constantly and even sold crocheted goods. I held classes one night a week and taught friends and relatives how to sew and crochet. I worked and visited friends. And I laughed when someone would help Rudy into the house because he had drank too much to walk.

My family had come and gone several times in those two and a half years. Currently Buzzie was off with some guy from the railroad, I was told. Howard had a bad accident some months before. While working on construction, and had lost three more fingers on that same hand with no thumb. He didn't keep his fingers pickled in a jar like he had his thumb so many years earlier.

The loss of most of his of his right hand was hard on Howard and Buzzie. She always wanted to do things for him and he wanted to learn how to do things himself. He would curse at her and say he could cut his own "blankety blank" meat, things like that. He had so much pain too. Sometimes he would say his finger nails felt dirty when of course he didn't have any finger nails.

Howard had several surgeries on that stump of a hand. It's strange that just as I'm writing about the hand accident I remember how he described the accident to me. He said he had been trying to link part of a section of a tall crane when the crane jumped onto his hand and took his fingers with it. He said he could see a man walking away and screaming but it was like it was someone else. I knew at the time exactly what he meant. For in the most painful moments of my life it had always seemed surreal to me too. Always like it was happening to someone else.

The last surgery on Howards hand didn't do much to improve the looks but it gave him a little grasping power. The doctor cut away the web between the thumb joint and in time he could bend that stump of a thumb over to meet the little finger. Soon he could even hold a cigarette and that was very important to him. Howard liked cigarettes about as much as Rudy liked beer.

The construction company paid Howard a big amount of money for losing his right hand. With the money he purchased forty acres of land that adjoined Sawyer Lake and was about twenty miles away from Antigo. Who knows maybe he wanted to return to his roots.

Buzzie said she could not live like that ever again and she refused to move with him. Howard moved up to his forty acres.

Punky had moved up with Howard for a while. First with his wife and after she ran away from them, he brought another woman in. The second women didn't run away but she made Punky find them a place of their own. Fredafaye and Punky settled into a shack close by Howard's place and were soon expecting a baby. Punky never got to see the baby be born though because the police came and drug him away and eventually sent him to Waupon State Prison. All these years I had thought it was for bigamy. I thought it was because he had married the second woman without divorcing the first one. Just recently people have told me Punky did more evil things than that. They say when him and Howard used to deliver furniture for the big stores they stole some for themselves and for friends too. If it is true, I wonder why Howard never went to jail? It is hard to know what is truth and what is fiction. But it is true that Punky was in Waupon State Prison for a couple of years. I went to see him once and it was a frightening place. I had made him a batch of cookies and the guards dumped them in the garbage can in front of us. It makes sense to me now that I am older and hopefully a little smarter. They can not take chances with prisoners that someone may be slipping them something in food. I never got to touch my brother in prison either. There was a glass wall between us.

It is my desire to keep the events on these pages as true and accurate as I possibly can. I firmly believe that people can control their own destiny. There are many people and many incidents that can influence you on your walk through this world but the ultimate person you become depends on what you grasp and keep from each. I know there is good and evil in everyone.

I know my brother had a lot of good in him. His heart was tender just like Howards. Maybe, just maybe he had done some dishonest things. Perhaps he had not learned that to take without asking was stealing. Maybe him and Howard were both crooked like people said. I don't know. I only know when he was sent to prison I could only think of good things about him. Punky nursing his dog Heinz back to health. Punky chasing the cows with me. Punky saving me from drowning one day on our trek to the lake for water, I had been leaning over with a milk can to fill it when I slipped and fell in, and big brother had pulled me out. Punky always trying to find food for us when both parents had left us alone. Punky and I dancing the "Hop" when we were in High School. Only loving memories in my mind. Now he was in prison and I couldn't see why. It was a hard time!

The guy.-- The guy was very close to the family and he had even paid room and to Rudy for a while. It was quite late on a week night and the guy called. He had problems and had to make decisions about work and his life, could he come and talk to Rudy and me about this and get our opinions. Rudy was working out of town. Oh, that's right the guy said, he had forgotten that. Well could he talk to me? He really needed to talk. Did I think it was strange at the time? I don't think I did. I think, if my memory serves me correctly, that it was kind of a prideful thing that this guy would want my advice. He was two years older than me and yet he thought I could advise him about his problems.

He brought beer and for hours we sat at the kitchen table discussing the world situation. When in that night did the conversation turn? I don't know. I came out from the bathroom once and he had the radio playing. We danced. He was sorry for how I was treated. He thought I was a wonderful person and that he had always cared for me. In retrospect I still don't know if the guy was worldly and it was all a calculated plan or if it was just poor judgement on both of our parts to be in that situation.

With daylight came guilt and confusion. What did it all mean? What would happen now? Was I becoming like Buzzie? Should I tell Rudy? Should I run away with my children and to where?

What would Ida and TJ think of their good little girl now? Questions, questions, questions. And no answers.

As it turned out I didn't have to do anything. The guy met Rudy at the bar and confessed because his conscience was killing him. Rudy was telling me all this and had a plan. He would forgive us both and it was not for punishment but for time, time to think and reflect on the whole sordid affair I guess. The children and I would go live with my father for a while. It would give him and me both time to think. It would be cheap and Rudy would save money. Then in a few months he would come get us and we would have a new beginning.

Late on a Friday night we arrived at Howard's. He was so happy to have us. He was frying fresh venison with onions and it smelled good in the cabin. I explored the place. It was good sized. There was a large kitchen with a small bedroom off to one side where the children and myself would sleep. The living room seemed huge and there was another bedroom off of it for Howard. Outside, close to the door was the pump. But where is the outhouse? I questioned. You have forty acres of trees out there said Howard, pick your spot. No wonder Buzzie and Punky's wife ran off. After living in the city for a while even an outhouse seemed hard to deal with and now Howard was saying there wasn't even an outhouse. He saw the look on my face and said he was going to make *a* new one. Apparently the old one fell apart when him and Punky tried to move it. I don't know if Howard ever make a new outhouse.

We settled into life with Howard and some things I remember fondly. If we walked along an old logging trail we would end up at the lake. The kids and I spent many hot days playing at the lake. Grandpa loved the kids and laughed quite often at and with them. At night some times he would talk of Buzzie and cry. He missed her so much. I missed her too.

Washing diapers was difficult at the cabin. I was used to washing by hand because the washing machine Buzzie had found in the paper had quit running before Michael had been born. I had been washing clothes in the bathtub for some time again but this was much more time consuming. First you had to find a spot to shake the solids out. Next you had to soak them in a pail of bleach water. On wash days you had to pump, haul, heat and then start the scrubbing in a wash tub. Reminiscent days of the farm from ten years earlier flooded my mind.

There was a little verse that would cross my mind a lot that summer. Just something I had congered up.

If Howard is a tree,
And Buzzie is a bee.
What species does that
make their offsprings.

There was more but it is long gone or distorted at least, from my mind. My mind was full of many worries and fears, like where the kids and I would end up and if my life would end up like my parents.

Oh yes, there were good times that summer. Howard would work in the woods sometimes, peeling poplar trees. Again reminiscent of the farm days for I could remember going with him and Punky on some occasions to cut down the tall trees and drag them back home with the horses. Lots of people in that area made money selling peeled Poplar trees. I told Howard I felt funny sometimes when he was gone, kind of afraid. He fixed that. A dog. Some friend of a friend had lots of dogs and soon we had one. Shang was a skinny and long haired dog of medium size and she was our friend and protector. The kids and I never went anywhere again without Shang.

Sometimes at dusk Howard would take us all down the country roads looking for deer. One particular night his car got struck in some deep logging ruts. We were a long way away from the cabin. He tried pushing while I drove. We put limbs and branches under the wheels, nothing helped. He was so sorry and sad but we would have to walk.

He figured if we cut across the plowed fields it would only be a few miles. My tall handsome Dad carrying little April and me with my hands locked together under Michael's butt we walked and we walked and we walked. It was farther than he had imagined and my hands and shoulders were numb. The ruts in the plowed fields were so deep. He felt so bad. It really wasn't so awful. At first we sang all our old songs and after a while the children fell asleep in our arms. We saw the cabin. He was so proud of how tough and uncomplaining I was. The next day he got a relative or friend to take him back for the car. They checked the mileage and said it had been almost ten miles that we had walked the night before.

Sometimes we would go into Antigo for supplies and over to see relatives. Those were enjoyable times. It had been years since I spent any time up north and it was good to see the relatives again. I was proud and happy for them to get to know my children now. They all agreed my children were not weeds, but nice, well mannered, well behaved little people. Proud? Yes, I was.

Rudy came up several times, usually with a car full of friends. The lake had outhouses and a nice picnic area. The friends would bring their sleeping bags or blankets and all sleep on the living room floor. I would make big kettles of barbecue out of venison or homemade pizza and it would be great fun. Mocky and Squeak both came to visit with Rudy and each of them stayed with us for a couple of weeks.

The summer was passing and one time I asked to go back for a visit. I would stay by my friend Donna's house. She wanted me to because she had written to say how much she missed me and the kids. Rudy didn't like the idea and spent hours telling me why. He wouldn't have the money to take me back to Howard's cabin in a week, he was afraid I would want to stay in Milwaukee, he didn't think he could trust me in Milwaukee and on and on. Howard stepped in. "Winter was coming" he said and the cabin was no place for me and the kids in the winter. Rudy was afraid that I really didn't miss him enough yet. He wanted me to promise him I would be a good girl and do what he said and to swear to him it was because I missed him we were coming back. It was a plan and a promise that I would say that to everyone. I promised!

The summer ended and the children and I went back to Milwaukee. Howard was alone now. How long he stayed up there alone I don't remember, but soon him and Buzzie were together and starting over again.

This new beginning didn't last long (they never did). Soon they were both heading in different directions. Buzzie had run off with some guy from the Railroad and Howard? Howard spent all his time crying. But lo and behold soon they were back together again. This time the two of them moved to Kenosha.

Soon Buzzie was encouraging me to leave Rudy again. She had been doing this for years. This time I listened! I called Howard and there was no hesitation. He would empty out a spare bedroom and get bunkbeds for the children and myself to sleep in. We stayed with them for two months, until we moved into our own, almost new apartment. It was wonderful!

Howard and Buzzie were both under doctor's care. Buzzie's cholesterol was high and Howard with constant Pleurisy. He was on permanent disability. They bought two little houses across the street from each other and they were always together. The only moving they did now was to move from little house to the other.

Howard doted on Buzzie. He shopped for and cooked her special food. He served her in bed and soon she got better. She had lost quite a bit of weight, she had always been on the plump side. She looked good!

Howard did not. He was going to the doctor a lot, and soon to the hospital for Chemo treatments.

On a cold Thursday in February we were all called. Howard's brothers and sisters all came down from Antigo. The doctor explained! Howard had coughed hard and his lungs, already weak from the Chemo treatments had ruptured.

They were able to stop the bleed temporarily But----. My illiterate, foul mouthed Father, my rescuer, my hero, my rock, my Daddy was gone. He was 59 years old.

Buzzie lived alone now for a few years, until she met and married George. He was Mocky's husband's widowed Father and soon Buzzie moved to Ohio with him to be by Mocky

What a twist of fate. Buzzie's new husband had a stroke shortly after they married, so now Buzzie had to care him night and day. She nursed George for several years until he passed away.

Alone again Buzzie was miserable. She didn't get out much, only when Mocky would pick her up and take her to the doctor. She thought of Howard all the time. When Buzzie passed away of a heart attack, a total of ten years after Howard's passing, we brought her body back to Kenosha and laid her by Howard's side. Perhaps they are having a New Beginning.

Howard & Buzzie in early 1970's

04160790-00955734

Printed in the United States
By Bookmasters